A GUIDE TO ANCIENT MEXICAN RUINS

by
C. Bruce Hunter

University of Oklahoma Press   Norman

By C. Bruce Hunter

A *Guide to Ancient Maya Ruins*. Norman, University of Oklahoma Press, 1974
A *Guide to Ancient Mexican Ruins*. Norman, University of Oklahoma Press, 1977

Library of Congress Cataloging in Publication Data

Hunter, C Bruce.
    A guide to ancient Mexican ruins.

    A companion volume to the author's A guide to ancient Maya ruins.
    Bibliography: p. 253
    Includes index.
    1. Indians of Mexico—Antiquities. 2. Mexico—
Antiquities. I. Title.
F1219.H922   972   76-62511
ISBN 0-8061-1399-5
ISBN 0-8061-1407-X pbk.

1P 1800
1st   750

A Guide to Ancient Mexican Ruins

To my daughter, Gail
with memories of our days at Mexican archaeological ruins

Preface

During the past twenty years, in leading archaeological field study trips to Mexico and the Maya areas for the Museum of Natural History and New York University, I have always been amazed that a good scholarly guide has not been written for these ancient ruins. This book and the companion to it, *A Guide to Ancient Maya Ruins*, are my sincere effort to fill the need for this type of guide.

It is difficult to write about ancient ruins without using technical jargon and a stack of statistics, but in this volume these have been kept at a minimum. My concern has been with the development of the ancient civilizations, how they functioned, and the importance of their works of art in architecture, sculpture, and minor crafts. I have noted especially the art styles and their influence by cross-cultural contact.

This *Guide to Ancient Mexican Ruins* does not include several important cultural areas either because ruins have not been found or excavation has not been carried out up to this time. Such areas as Tres Zapotes, La Venta, and San Lorenzo are extremely significant Olmec sites on the Gulf coastal plain. Even if one goes there, there is very little to see. This is also true of the West Coast cultural areas of Colima, Guerrero, Nayarit, and Jalisco. Others could also be mentioned. It is fortunate that some of the great treasures from these cultures are housed in museums. The Maya areas of southern Mexico are not included in this book since that area is dealt with under a separate cover.

Acknowledgments are extremely difficult, for any writer is indebted to many people for research and for technical and editorial assistance. I am especially grateful to Gloria Davis for reading my manuscript and making editorial suggestions. I also would like to thank Norman Mathews for patiently reading my notes and typing the manuscript. Never a year goes by that my students have not called my attention to some discovery they have made that I have not noticed. To these students, and to the many stimulating people who have participated in the field study trips, I would like to offer my gratitude for their suggestions, inspirations, and enthusiasm. I am especially grateful to Merle and Glema Mahr, Fred Bove, and David Jones for their enduring friendship and encouragement over the years.

C. BRUCE HUNTER

New York City
January 6, 1977

Contents

Black-and-White Illustrations

A *Guide to Ancient Mexican Ruins*

xiv

*Unless otherwise credited, all photographs
were made by the author.*

Color Plates

Maps and Plans

A Guide to Ancient Mexican Ruins

I Introduction

The first evidence of early man in Mexico is still uncertain, but indications of habitation extend back prior to 8000 B.C. It is quite possible that man's first arrival may have been as early as ten or twenty thousand years before this time. He is known to have hunted large mammals such as mammoths, but probably had a heartier diet of rabbits, birds, turtles, fish, deer, and other small game. This food was supplemented with wild plants, especially beans, peppers, squash, fruits, tubers, and bulbs. With the disappearance of big game and the tremendous increase in population, tribal peoples, organized into hunting bands, had to rely on a more basic food source, and agriculture soon was to develop in the fertile valleys. Some of the earliest types of agricultural villages were established between 5000 and 2000 B.C. along lake fronts and riverbeds. At this time fruits and vegetables such as avocados, beans, squash, and a host of other plants were cultivated. Corn was cultivated as early as 4000 B.C. in the southeast Pueblo area according to excavations carried out by Richard S. MacNeish in 1960. Stone jars and bowls were first used for utilitarian purposes until the firing of clay was discovered, approximately 2300 B.C. in Mexico, and ceramic bowls were then used. However, the making of large stone bowls did continue into Classic times.

Larger village settlements were on the increase by 2000 B.C., which marks the beginning of the Early Preclassic period. This formative period continued until 1200 B.C. by which time there were a number of important village sites on the Plateau of Mexico near Lake Texcoco that have been significant in the cultural development of Mexico. These were El Arbolillo, Tlatilco, Zacatenco, Copilco, and Tlapacoya. At this time a great number of female figurines, crudely made in gingerbread style, began to appear all over Mesoamerica, indicating

3

the possibility of an extensive fertility cult. Who the people were who occupied the valley and where they came from is unknown. Their tools, which met their needs for agriculture, were the digging stick, stone axes, hoes, and other shaped tools from stones, bones, and wood. Body adornment was popular during this early time, even though clothes were sparse. Most figurines found from this period indicate no clothing except in a few instances when a small skirt or a loincloth was worn.

During the Middle Preclassic period 1200–600 B.C. there was great activity over a large part of Mesoamerica in town planning, trade, and the control of territory by hereditary chiefs. There is some indication of a class-structured society at this time, the creation of multiple deities, the beginnings of glyphic writing, mathematics, and an understanding of astronomy that made a seasonal calendar possible. A number of older towns, such as Tlatilco, Tlapacoya, Copilco, and Zacatenco, continued to function. However, great numbers of new towns and villages were now emerging all over Mesoamerica, and warring chiefs were engaging in skirmishes for political control of larger areas of choice lands. It is quite possible that trade contact with South America existed. At the site of Tlatilco, many stirrup-spout jars, a typical pottery form in Peru, have been found.

During the Middle Preclassic period one great civilization in Mesoamerica became extremely important. This was the Olmec. The Olmec heartland was on the Veracruz coast, where three large cities set the pattern for cultural development: La Venta, Tres Zapotes, and San Lorenzo. In these cities were pyramids and temples to honor their gods, plazas for their ceremonies, large populations of people organized into a structured society of priests and rulers, merchants, craftsmen, and farmers. Honoring the gods and the dead was a critical part of the Olmecs' thinking. For this reason tomb accessories and sculptures of the elite and their deities were essential for dignifying these traditions.

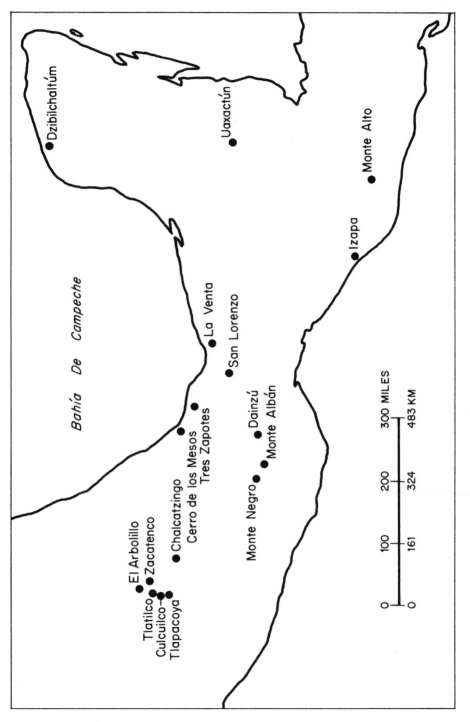

Preclassic Cultures

Dzibilchaltúm

Uaxactún

Monte Alto

Izapa

Bahía De Campeche

La Venta

San Lorenzo

Tres Zapotes

Cerro de los Mesos

Chalcatzingo

El Arbolillo

Zacatenco

Tlatilco

Culcuilco

Tlapacoya

Dainzú

Monte Negro

Monte Albán

0   100   200   300 MILES

0   161   324   483 KM

The choice of the lowlands of the Gulf coastal plain was important, for this area had fertile soil, plenty of rainfall the year around, tropical temperatures for continuous crop cycles, the coast and river areas for transportation to other markets, and enough luxury items to create competition with other cultural areas. The influence of the Olmecs in other far-flung cities of Mesoamerica was enormous. Areas as far south as El Salvador and Honduras, west to Guerrero, and as far north as Tlatilco were to come under their patronage or their control. The archaeological site of La Venta, situated on an island in the Tonala River, is best known for the gigantic sculptured heads now located in the La Venta Park at Villahermosa. In style these large sculptures have simple curving forms, little ornamentation, and are on a monumental scale regardless of the size of the sculpture, with a predominance of large heads, altars, stelae, and narrative boulder reliefs. The jaguar and possibly the serpent seem to be the only religious expression in animal form. Anthropomorphic sculptures of the jaguar and man are so common there is a general belief the jaguar may have been the totem animal of the ruling families of the Olmec.[1] Others hold that the jaguar and man or woman cohabited in legendary times and that this was the beginning of the Olmec people. The anthropomorphic jaguar-man sculptures have several features in common: the cleft forehead, flamelike eyebrows, snarling lips, a "baby face," toothless gums, and sometimes curving fangs and claws. The body shows no sex differentiation.

Burials in caches and tombs have revealed handsome carvings in precious stones, especially jades. The jades are so highly polished they resemble smooth, glistening gems as though covered with water. No people throughout history, using only stone, wood, and bone tools, have brought jade to

---

[1]*An interesting new book by a historian of religions, Karl W. Luckert, proposes that it was a serpent, rather than the commonly represented jaguar, that was the religious symbol of the Olmecs* (Olmec Religion: A Key to Middle America and Beyond [*Norman, University of Oklahoma Press, 1976*]).

The strong sculptural quality of the Olmec style is noted in this dramatic depiction of a monkey or monkey deity. This sculpture was originally located at La Venta, but has been removed to the La Venta Park in Villahermosa. Middle Preclassic.

Monument 4, La Venta Park, Villahermosa. A group of colossal heads were carved by the Olmecs at La Venta, Tres Zapotes, and San Lorenzo. The source of the basalt for Olmec carving was approximately eighty miles north of this area. Middle Preclassic.

such a high polish. This precious stone, in shades of blue-gray, green, and white, was used by the Olmecs for beads, earplugs, wrist and leg bands, shallow dishes for anointing the body with powders and oils, adzes for ceremonial use, deities, and full figure or head portraits of people of the time. Such a luxury item as jade was traded over a large part of Mesoamerica. One of the finest of these pieces is the large ceremonial adze of blue-gray jade, believed to have come from the Oaxaca area, now located in The American Museum of Natural History in New York. Two of the great collections of Olmec jade are in the same museum, which has a superb group of the blue-gray jades, and at the Museo Nacional de Antropologia e Historia in Mexico City, which has an excellent group of the green jades as well as many other pieces.

Because of the intrusion of the oil companies at La Venta, most of the great sculptures were moved to Villahermosa, where they are now located in an open-air park. Some of the large Olmec sculptures from San Lorenzo, Tres Zapotes, Laguna de los Cerros, and other centers in Veracruz also have been moved from their sites and are now located in an open-air park at Jalapa.

Important sites showing Olmec influence are located in other regional areas of Mexico outside of the Olmec heartland on the Veracruz coast. These would include the Tlatilco site north of Mexico City, the Chalcatzingo reliefs in eastern Morelos, and the Juxtlahuaca cave paintings in Guerrero. Centuries after the Olmec cities were abandoned, their style continued along the Veracruz coastal plain, across the Tehuantepec Isthmus, into the Oaxaca Valley, and along the Guatemala coastal plain.

During Middle and Late Preclassic times other non-Olmec ceremonial centers were also functioning, producing outstanding architectural forms, sculpture, and ceramic art. Of these, Monte Albán and Dainzú are especially important in the Oaxaca Valley, Copilco and Cuicuilco in the Mexican plateau, the Maya sites in the southern region of Mesoamerica, Cerro de los Mesas in the Veracruz coast, and Izapa in Chiapas. The art style of Izapa is derived from the Olmec, but differs from it in the use of decorative baroque-styled compositions. This style is closely related to the Maya, which quite obviously must have influenced it as Maya-styled monuments have been found

9

Wooden mask, originally encrusted with jade decoration, found in a cave in Guerrero. Olmec. Middle Preclassic. Courtesy The American Museum of Natural History, New York.

along the coastal plain of Guatemala and into the highlands.

During the Classic Period (A.D. 300–900) four vast civilizations were to emerge in Mesoamerica, all within a few centuries of each other. The most important of these was that of the Mayas, who controlled the territory from Honduras and El Salvador through Guatemala and Belize and north to Yucatán and southern Mexico. Teotihuacán was the most important of the northern civilizations, with an empire that was influential as far south as Kaminaljuy, Guatemala. It is quite possible the great city of Cholula was also part of this empire. The third magnificent civilization of Mesoamerica during the

10

Detail of Stela 3, La Venta Park, Villahermosa. This important Olmec dignitary, beautifully carved in stone relief, is part of a large monument in narrative style. Middle Preclassic.

11

Classic period is that of Monte Albán, controlled by the Zapotecs. The fourth of these great civilizations is the Veracruz Classic civilization.

The Classic period is the Golden Age when some of the greatest cities were built in the Americas, leaving us a heritage of imposing palaces, spectacular temple-pyramids, great plazas, and other noble structures. Seemingly the people of this time were at relative peace with the existing power blocs. Energies were being expended on cultural development rather than warfare. Great luxury goods were being created, and the arts had reached an extraordinarily fine florescence. It was a time of scientific development in astronomy and mathematics, and glyph writing reached a peak with the Mayas. These Classic civilizations were to set the pattern and were to influence all future cultural developments until the Spanish Conquest.

For a short time in Mesoamerican history, between the Classic and Postclassic periods, large groups of tribal peoples under powerful chieftains competed for territorial rights as the old Classic sites were abandoned. This turbulent period is now referred to as the Terminal Classic period (A.D. 700–900). During this time there was much activity in the Valley of Mexico, where the Mixtecs and Toltecs were on the ascendancy.

The Postclassic period (A.D. 900–1520) was dominated by two major empires in Mexico. First, the Toltecs established a powerful empire with a capital at Tula in the Early Postclassic phase (A.D. 900–1200). Their control was felt as far south as Yucatán, where the Toltecs ruled a second capital city, Chichén Itzá. The Toltecs were characterized as a warring people desirous of controlling extensive territories and by eclecticism in architecture and other art forms. Yet in some phases of their arts, they possessed vigor, creativity, and great craftsmanship.

The Late Postclassic phase (A.D. 1200–1520) saw the rise of yet another warlike empire, the Aztec. The Aztec capital city at Tenochtitlán was to dazzle the explorers of the new world when Cortés landed in 1520, and it also was to shock peoples ever after because of the Aztecs' insatiable thirst for

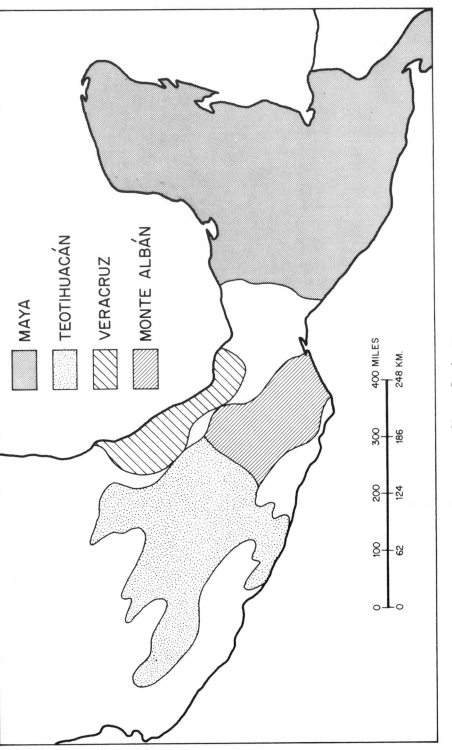

MAYA

TEOTIHUACÁN

VERACRUZ

MONTE ALBÁN

0   100   200   300   400 MILES

0   62   124   186   248 KM.

Classic Civilizations

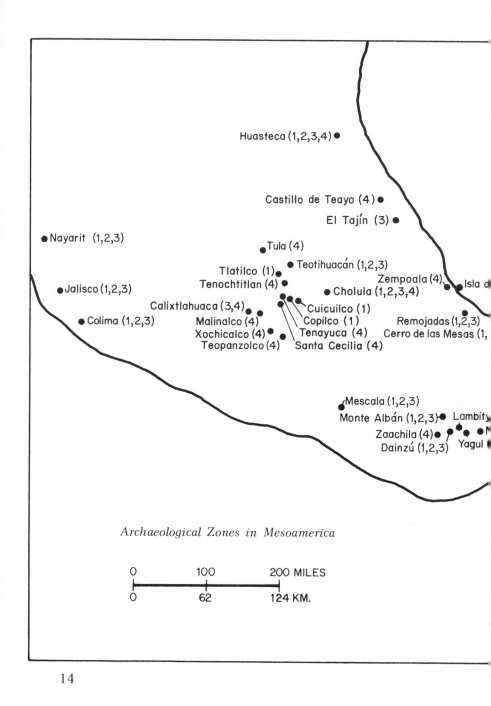

Huasteca (1,2,3,4) ●

Castillo de Teayo (4) ●

El Tajín (3) ●

● Nayarit (1,2,3)

● Tula (4)

Tlatilco (1) ● ● Teotihuacán (1,2,3)
Tenochtitlan (4) ●
● Jalisco (1,2,3)
Zempoala (4) ●
● Isla d
● Cholula (1,2,3,4)

Calixtlahuaca (3,4) ● ● Cuicuilco (1)
● Colima (1,2,3)
Malinalco (4) ● ● Copilco (1)
Remojadas (1,2,3)
Xochicalco (4) ● ● Tenayuca (4)
Cerro de las Mesas (1,
Teopanzolco (4) ● Santa Cecilia (4)

● Mescala (1,2,3)
Monte Albán (1,2,3) ● ● Lambity
Zaachila (4) ● ● ● ●
Dainzú (1,2,3) Yagul ●

Archaeological Zones in Mesoamerica

0	100	200 MILES
0	62	124 KM.

Dzibilchaltún (1,2,3,4)
Izamal (3,4) Chichén Itzá (3,4)
Acancéh (3,4) Cobá (3)
Mayapán (4) Tulum (4)
Uxmal (3)
Jaina (3) Kabah (3)
Labná (3)
Sayil (3)
Xlapak (3)
Etzna (3)

icios (4)

Santa Rita de Corozal (4)

Caminalcalco (3)
Zapotes (1) Uaxactún (1,2,3)
La Venta (1)
an Lorenzo (1) Tikal (1,2,3)
Palenque (3)
Piedras Negras (3)
Tonina (3) Yaxchilán (3)
Chiapas de Bonampak (3) Seibal (1,2,3)
) Corzo (1,2)
Alter de Sacrificios (1,2,3)

Nebaj (3) Quiriguá (3)
Zaculeu (3,4)
Izapa (1) Mixco Viejo (4) Copán (3)
El Baúl (3) Kaminaljuyú (1,2,3)
Monte Alto (1)
El Bilbao
Tazumal (3)

15

human sacrifice. It should be remembered, however, that within the context of the Aztec civilization and within the traditions of the people, sacrifice was an honorable way of meeting death. The Aztec civilization produced an extraordinary group of craftsmen, the most outstanding being sculptors. Both the heroic sculptures, with all their vigorous force and power, and the smaller animal sculptures of snakes, grasshoppers, coyotes, and jaguars are among the great masterpieces in any world of art.

The archaeological zones that we see today in Mexico are only a skeletal expression of the total dynamic force engendered by these master civilizations. Most of the architecture and much of the sculpture are buried under the ground with centuries of earth over them. Some cultural areas did not produce great city builders. This was true in the Chiapas, Huasteca, Guerrero, and other regions farther north. However, these areas have produced some of the most remarkable works of art in small sculptures and ceramics.

Archaeologists in the years ahead will be uncovering many more of the large cities and great treasures produced by the indigenous people of the Americas, the Indians. These new excavations should help piece together the great voids in phases of individual cultures, and give us a clearer insight into the significance of cultural evolution in Mesoamerica.

II Valley of Mexico

Cuicuilco and Copilco

The volcano, representing the inner forces of the earth, the earth gods, the Lords of the Night, and the deities associated with darkness, has had a mystic force in the internal structure of ancient American cultures. Both Copilco and Cuicuilco were partially buried when this region felt the pulsating tremors and thrusts of spurting lava from the volcanic cone of Xitle in the misty mountain range of Ajusco located just a few miles from the center of present-day Mexico City. The brutal eruption took place in Late Preclassic times, preserving forever a tremendous ceremonial center and its culture—an island in a riverbed of lava. It was found in excavating the area of these ruins that the lava was as much as twenty-five feet deep in places.

Copilco is the earlier site and dates from the Middle Preclassic period (1200–400 B.C.). It had already been abandoned at the time Xitle erupted. Cuicuilco, however, was still occupied, and many flourishing cultural activities were in progress when people of the city were terrified by the advancing red molten lava.

Copilco and Cuicuilco were commercial and religious centers for large farm communities stretching far into the countryside. The political organization may have been similar to that of city-states. It is quite possible rule was theocratic, headed by a priestly order. Many deities have been found at both sites. Such a large ceremonial center would imply a dense population in these urban areas, which must have had a high degree of social organization in which class distinctions were possible. Copilco was not the only influential center in the Mexican plateau in Middle Preclassic times. Other centers of culture were Tlatilco, active from the earliest of Preclassic times, El Arbolillo, Zacatenco, Tlapacoya, and Coatepec, to mention a few. Even though the villagers of these centers were agricultural people, they still depended to a great degree on fishing, hunting, and gathering. Wild fruits, bulbs, grasses, and herbs were a part of the diet. Corn was the basis of their economy and their most important food reserve. Among their more advanced technology was the development of hydraulic agriculture, which correlates with the growth of large urban centers. However, it is most likely that a variety of agricultural systems was being used during this Late Preclassic period. Stone, bone, and wood tools were arduously worked to fashion implements of daily life such as manos and metates for grinding corn, awls, scrapers, projectile points, and many other instruments. Full-time craft specialization was already a part of community activities. Dwellings were of perishable materials, but stone foundations were not uncommon. They were small one- or two-room structures, using pole, wattle-and-daub, adobe, or stone walls. Roofing was thatch or wood. Materials for construction were obtained from local sources, depending for the most part on environmental conditions. In pine forest areas at higher altitudes, wood was abundant for construction. However, in the valleys where forests had long since disappeared, natural grasses had to be used for thatching.

Hand-modeled figurines were extremely popular and have been sometimes associated with burial rituals. Some of these burials can be seen under the lava flow at the Copilco site in tunnels dug into the pyramid by archaeologists. In this area persons were buried in an extended position with a few of their belongings, jars of food, amulets, and tokens for passage into the underworld.

The major pyramid at Cuicuilco is circular, as were many early structures in Preclassic times. Preclassic pottery from the Guerrero region of western Mexico depicts circular towers or pyramids having many platforms that we can assume typify temples or shrines. A fluted circular pyramid at La Venta on

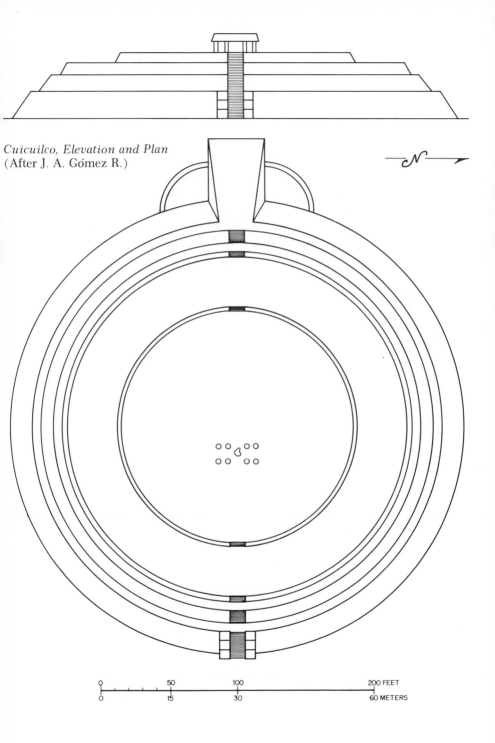

Cuicuilco, Elevation and Plan
(After J. A. Gómez R.)

0	50	100		200 FEET
0	15	30		60 METERS

The great circular pyramid at Cuicuilco was originally faced with stone and set in clay. The ramp approach faces north. Late Preclassic.

the Gulf coastal plain was being used by the Olmecs in the Middle Preclassic period (1500–600 B.C.). Under the circular pyramid at Cuicuilco is an earlier circular structure constructed of mud. There is some indication that the facing stones were removed by the Cuicuilco people themselves to be used for other structures. There may have been several enlargements of the great pyramid before it reached its present shape. The first two platforms of the pyramid may date from as early as the fifth century B.C. Two additional platforms were added sometime between the third and second centuries B.C. The base of the pyramid is approximately 370 feet, and the pyramid rises in four conical platforms reaching a height of 60 feet. Large, smooth river boulders as well as andesite stones were used over the earthen core to face the platforms. As early as the first millennium B.C., earth, rock, rubble, and adobe were being used to build homes, temples, palaces, and pyramids.

Detail of the Cuicuilco pyramid showing the platforms. In Late Pre-classic times this pyramid was partially buried by a volcanic flow. Archaeologists have dug to the base of the pyramid, creating a trench. Late Preclassic.

It was not until the beginning of the Christian era that cut stone and lime mortar was used.

The approach to the pyramid, oriented to the cardinal points, is from the east. This orientation alone is enough to make us aware of the importance of astronomy to the early peoples in this valley. Through astronomy they could regulate the planting and harvest seasons and determine other important dates and times in their calendar. Both the lower east and west sides of the pyramid had great ramps constructed as the approach to the first terrace. Succeeding terraces had stairways. At the top of the pyramid are a number of super-

21

imposed elliptical altars of compressed earth faced with large stones. At one time the altars were painted red — a color popularly used throughout Mesoamerica as far south as the Maya area. Neither mortar nor limestone was used at this time.

An unusual small structure that may have been a shrine is located at the southeast side of the pyramid base. Large stone slabs, inclining inward and arranged in a circle, form a single chamber with an opening left for a doorway. This structure was covered by additional stone slabs to form a roof. On the inside of the chamber are the remains of a mural type of decoration consisting of red curving lines that may have represented symbolic or realistic objects such as snakes and lizards. A reproduction of this structure can be seen at the Museum of Anthropology (Museo Nacional de Antropologia e Historia) in Mexico City.

Surrounding the great pyramid of Cuicuilco is a deep channel in the lava, dug out by archaeologists in order to expose the base of the pyramid. Because of the difficulty in digging through the lava to discover what lies beneath, excavations here will be few in the years to come.

Adjacent to the ruins is a small museum that houses artifacts from the site as well as a few from other areas dating from Preclassic times. One of the most important gods in Mexico, the "fire god" or "old god," can be seen here. He is represented in a seated, stooped position with a large brazier resting on his back. His face is wrinkled and his mouth is toothless. This deity was first depicted during the Late Preclassic period and is here represented at Cuicuilco. Every succeeding civilization in Mexico down to the Aztec honored this deity and included him in their pantheon of venerable objects.

Cuicuilco, saddened by the ravages of time, may seem of little consequence to the traveler viewing this mound today. However, it was here that the stage was set for the style of future ceremonial centers. It was here that specialization in crafts fostered competition that inspired artists to create greater masterpieces, and it was here that patterns were set for political rule and religious activities. Preclassic sites such as Cuicuilco, Monte Albán I and II, Izapa, and Cerro de las Mesas were to prepare the way for the great Classic renaissance in the Valley of Mexico and the Gulf coastal plain. For most centers in the central highlands the renaissance started at the beginning of the Christian era.

Teotihuacán Architecture

The largest city in the Americas, much larger than most European cities of the time, was the ancient Classic city of Teotihuacán. At its height in the seventh century, the city may have had a population of from 75,000 to 125,000. It is possible, however, that the population may have been much larger if apartments were occupied to their maximum capacity. This would raise the number to 200,000 persons, according to estimates made by René Millon. The plan of the city is compact and nucleated, arranged in grids on a north-south axis, with avenues and streets separating more-or-less-square blocks, covering an area of approximately eight square miles. The focal point of the city is the Pathway of the Dead, given that name by the Spaniards, as they thought the large earthen mounds along the Pathway were burial mounds. With recent excavation, these mounds proved to be the palace structures and temples. However, the name "Pathway of the Dead" is still with us. It was probably a great ceremonial highway in its day, as it was planned on a grand scale with a total length of two miles. Starting at the Pyramid of the Moon, this avenue extends well beyond the Ciudadela to the south.

The greatest concentration of people in the city was in the northwestern sector, and from its earliest time this may well have been the old quarter of the city. It was an area that housed city specialists such as craftsmen and merchants. Surveys indicate more than five hundred artisan workshops in the ancient city. Nevertheless, most of the population was engaged in farming. At times the people could be called upon as laborers for city construction and the many other tasks required of a class-structured society. Of the many workshops discovered

Teotihuacán. The Pathway of the Dead with the Plaza of the Moon in the foreground and the Pyramid of the Sun in the distance. Protoclassic.

by archaeologists, most were for working obsidian. Others specialized in ceramic figurines, utilitarian objects, and different types of stonework. Most structures in the city were of one story and formed compounds not unlike those in parts of rural Mexico today.

Between the first and second centuries major construction began at Teotihuacán on the Pyramid of the Sun, the highest of the pyramids in Mesoamerica north of the Maya area. From ancient times a small shrine was in this location, and when the Pyramid of the Sun was constructed, the sun-dried clay-

24

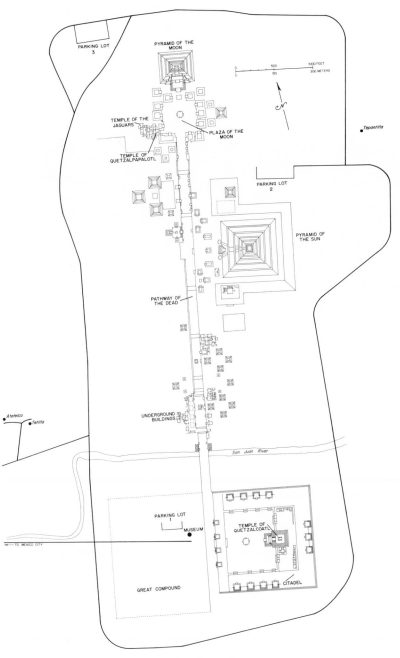

PARKING LOT
3

PYRAMID OF THE
MOON

500   1000 FEET
50   300 METERS

N

• Tepantitla

TEMPLE OF THE
JAGUARS

PLAZA OF THE
MOON

TEMPLE OF
QUETZALPAPALOTL

PARKING LOT
2

PYRAMID OF
THE SUN

PATHWAY OF
THE DEAD

• Atetelco
• Tetitla

UNDERGROUND
BUILDINGS

San Juan River

PARKING LOT
1

MUSEUM

TEMPLE OF
QUETZALCOATL

→ TO MEXICO CITY

GREAT COMPOUND

CITADEL

Teotihuacán

Pyramid of the Sun, Teotihuacán, second tallest pyramid in the Americas, is 110 feet to the top platform. Protoclassic period.

brick core was constructed over this shrine. The base of the pyramid is as large as that of Cheops in Egypt, but it is not as tall. In 1905, Leopoldo Batres was in charge of reconstructing the pyramid and, unfortunately, made an error in rebuilding the platforms. There should be four great platforms rather than the five that now exist. The surface of these platforms is completely covered with volcanic stones set in cement. Protruding from this surface are stone projections which originally held the very thick surface of plaster rigid. With the addition of a temple on top of the Pyramid of the Sun, the height may have been close to that of Temple IV at Tikal, which towers

26

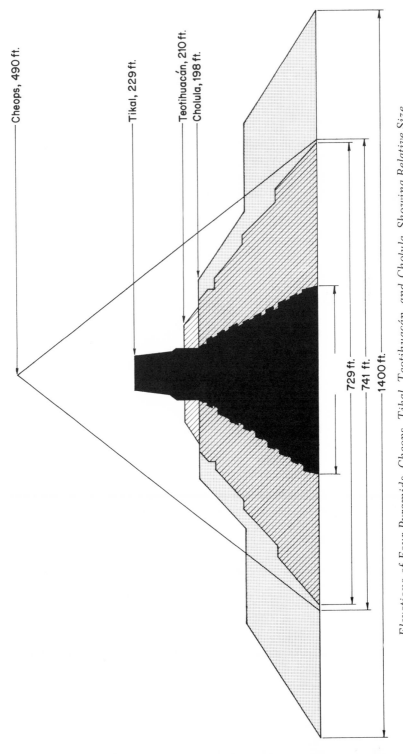

Cheops, 490 ft.

Tikal, 229 ft.

Teotihuacán, 210 ft.

Cholula, 198 ft.

729 ft.

741 ft.

1400 ft.

Elevations of Four Pyramids, Cheops, Tikal, Teotihuacán, and Cholula, Showing Relative Size

229 feet above the jungle floor in the Petén and is the tallest such structure in the Americas. Like most ceremonial centers throughout Mesoamerica, Teotihuacán is oriented to the cardinal points. The Pyramid of the Sun, the first large construction here, may have decided the axis of the city. It faces west with a deviation of 17 degrees, and is so placed that on the day the sun passes the zenith, it is directly in front of the monument.

A major excavation and reconstruction program was initiated at Teotihuacán between 1962 and 1964 by the Instituto Nacional de Antropologia e Historia. It employed 1,500 workmen and 8 archaeologists under the direction of Ignacio Bernal. This program accomplished a tremendous feat, executed in just two years, bringing to light the great palace and temple structures along the Pathway of the Dead, and revealing the illustrious murals found in many of the palace and temple rooms.

The tremendous mound of earth that represented the Pyramid of the Moon was excavated at this time, revealing a pyramid of great beauty. The interlocking truncated pyramidal volumes that make up the façade are admirably conceived. In the late afternoon light the play of shadow suggests the vigor, the power, and the massiveness of this imposing structure. The Pyramid of the Moon has four enormous platforms which at one time supported a temple building, but none exists today. The Pyramid of the Moon is just 116 feet high, but because the elevation of the ceremonial center is higher at the north end, the top of the Pyramid of the Sun and Moon are the same. Facing south, the Pyramid of the Moon commands a view of the city and dominates the surrounding architecture. Directly in front of this pyramid is the Plaza of the Moon, a highly formalized arrangement of twelve temple platforms surrounding a plaza approximately four acres square. Here, as well as along the Pathway of the Dead, the buildings were constructed in two separate time periods. The additions made during later times were placed between the existing structures. In the center of the plaza is a low platform that could have been used as a multiple-purpose structure for

Pyramid of the Moon, Teotihuacán, located at the north end of the Pathway of the Dead. Protoclassic.

pageantry, for religious incantations, or for the placement of basins of oil that, when lighted, would give a mystifying quality to the area. In the southwest corner of the plaza is located the newly reconstructed Palace of Quetzalpapalotl and the Palace of the Jaguars.

When one looks down the Pathway of the Dead, the consistent regularity of the architectural style becomes obvious. In this series of many platforms, the *talud-tablero* is the dominant motif. (The *talud* is the sloping base, the *tablero* the vertical paneled plane above the *talud*.) The low *talud* acts as a base for each of the tableroed platforms. And each *tablero* became an area that the artists could utilize for painting murals or for sculpture. This style of architecture was so impressive that it was soon employed by architects at El Tajín, Monte Albán, Cholula, and many other sites during Classic time. Notwithstanding, these architects were inventive enough to

Pyramid of the Moon, Teotihuacán. Beautifully conceived volumes forming the platforms of the pyramid makes this structure an architectural masterpiece. Protoclassic.

adapt both the *talud* and *tablero* in many different ways so that each of their architectural cities has an individual look.

The platforms along the Pathway of the Dead supported temples, palaces and some administrative buildings. No structures are here today, but there are foundations of some of the building walls. These can be seen by climbing to the top of some of the structures along the famous "pathway." In some of the palaces along the Pathway of the Dead are still preserved many of the splendid murals at Teotihuacán. As I pointed out earlier, this ceremonial highway, one of the most splendid in ancient Mexico, may have been used for great religious

30

Palace of Quetzalpapalotl, Teotihuacán. The entrance stairway and portico to the left and the platformed structure to the right are typical architectonic features at Teotihuacán. In the latter can be seen the popular tectonic device, the talud *and* tablero. *Classic period.*

ceremonies. It could have been a regal esplanade for coronations of rulers and chiefs. And it was an avenue of great dimension to serve the daily needs of this city.

A colossal basalt statue of the Water Goddess, Chalchiuhtlicue, was found near the Pyramid of the Moon. This sculpture has a small pectoral cavity in the location of the heart. A few other sculptures here and in the Huasteca area show this same cavity, but this sculpture is one of the earliest examples of it. It is reported that such cavities had a stone heart inserted, possibly suggesting the soul, the power, or the inner force of the goddess. Because of its flat-topped headdress and the mas-

31

Chalchiuhlicue, Goddess of Water, is represented in this colossal basalt sculpture located in front of the Museum of Anthropology in Mexico City. A smaller sculpture of the Goddess of Water, found next to the Pyramid of the Moon, is located inside the museum.

sive, geometric shape, it may have been used as an Atlantean figure to support a lintel, in the manner of the Toltecs in Postclassic times. The largest sculpture of this goddess, never completed, is now located in front of the Museum of Anthropology in Mexico City.

With the constant and ongoing cross-cultural contact of the major civilizations of the time, Teotihuacán surely influenced Monte Albán and El Tajín. This is noted in ceramics, sculpture, and painting. A very beautiful, extremely thin orange pottery was made in abundance in the Teotihuacán area and shipped to all parts of Mesoamerica as a trade item. Another of the distinctive pottery types is the cylinder-shaped, tripodal vase. This elegant pottery was often decorated with exquisite fresco paintings that were applied after the pottery was fired. The Mayas at Tikal were especially fond of this trade item and adopted the design for their use. The Tikal vases are a little taller than those at Teotihuacán and sometimes have four legs. Another source of wealth at Teotihuacán was obsidian, which was fashioned into tools and traded into other areas.

Toward the south end of the Pathway of the Dead are two of the largest compounds at Teotihuacán. The Cuidadela, or Citadel, is on the east side of this avenue, and the Great Compound is on the west. This area of the city, according to René Millon, was the bureaucratic and commercial center. The Great Compound was the city's largest, and consisted of two raised platforms with structures that were secular in nature. This imposing plaza could have been the major commercial marketplace for the city. Today this general area houses a museum, gift shops, and a parking lot.

The Citadel was probably the political center of the city. Theocratic rule at this time may have been both religious and secular. Therefore, the area of the Citadel probably had some temples and residences for the priests. The Citadel's great plaza is surrounded by large platforms on the four sides which enclose it completely. These platforms support a series of isolated pyramids that originally had superstructures. A stairway over the west platform leads to the great sunken plaza and the Pyramid of Quetzalcoatl, the most important structure here. In front of this pyramid is a pyramid structure with four platforms. Explorations proved that this structure was actually covering the much earlier Pyramid of Quetzalcoatl. The first of these was built in the third century, and the late structure is probably from the fifth century. When archaeologists excavated the Pyramid of Quetzalcoatl, only part of it still remained—the first four platforms of the façade and the staircase. Originally there were six platforms. The style of architecture is typical of Teotihuacán in that the *talud* and *tablero* are the dominant forms for the pyramid. The *tableros* are unique in that they frame beautifully carved sculptures of Tláloc, the Rain God, and the Plumed Serpent. These two sculptured deities alternate within the *tablero*. Between the meandering serpents' bodies are seashell sculptures of scallops, conches, and olive shells. Vestiges of plaster and red paint are still visible on some of the sculpture. All the sculptures are related to the water and fertility cults, and this temple may have been dedicated to these deities. On either side of the stairway is a balustrade with sculptured serpent heads placed at intervals. The Pyramid of Quetzalcoatl is one of the marvelous creations of architects at a time before Teotihuacán reached its ultimate florescence.

Teotihuacán structures are composed of many superimpositions from the beginning of these Indians' bulding programs, possibly as early as 100 B.C., until the destruction and abandonment of their city toward the end of the seventh century. One of the subterranean superimpositions that can be seen by the visitor is that of the Underground Buildings. These chambers were not built to be underground, but, instead, other structures were built on top of them. Today we can go down a stairway and see the type of construction used for temples. Here is an ancient well and other architectural details that were common during the first few centuries.

In ancient Mexico the Teotihuacán civilization was extremely important in effecting change on other cultures. Far-

Cylinder-shaped tripod vase, Teotihuacán, elegantly shaped and decorated in low relief with interlocking designs. Classic period. Courtesy The American Museum of Natural History.

away areas such as Dzibilchaltún and Acancéh in Yucatán, and Kaminaljuyú and Tikal in Guatemala were highly influenced by Teotihuacán in their architecture as well as in their minor crafts. It is even quite possible Kaminaljuyú was a secondary capital, controlling economic and commercial interests between Guatemala and Teotihuacán. The Classic Teotihuacán civilization left a tremendous art legacy and a great

35

Stairway to the Pyramid of Quetzalcoatl, Teotihuacán. The ramps on either side of the stairway are decorated with plumed serpent heads. Classic period.

architectural heritage to the people of all succeeding centuries as well as that of our own time.

Teotihuacán Murals

When the rainy season comes to a close, the Valley of Mexico shimmers in a cloak of green vegetation—a valley where months earlier the gray, parched earth seemed like a barren, hopeless land. It is then that one is aware how rich this valley is for agriculture. The tremendous size of the valley for production, the water systems for irrigation and transportation, and the possibility of accommodating a large population were fundamental to the birth of a civilization. In Preclassic times the Valley of Mexico was already highly involved in a cultural

36

Detail of the plumed serpent head that decorates the ramp of the stairway to the Pyramid of Quetzalcoatl. Classic period.

development that was to be the foundation for the beginning of the great Mesoamerican civilization of Teotihuacán. This civilization was to produce some of the most dazzling murals in pre-Conquest America.

Désiré Charnay was the first European to report finding the Teotihuacán murals. The year was 1888. Shortly after this time Leopoldo Bates uncovered murals in the Temple of Agriculture. More recently, between 1962 and 1964, many new murals were discovered during the excavation of mounds along the Pathway of the Dead. At this time restoration of many of the murals was undertaken. The large palace-type structures, some having more than fifty rooms with numerous patios and courtyards, were completely painted with murals.

Detail of the façade to the Pyramid of Quetzalcoatl. The platforms are decorated with the water deity, Tláloc, and the plumed serpent. Between the undulations of the serpent are conch, scallop, and olive seashells. Classic period.

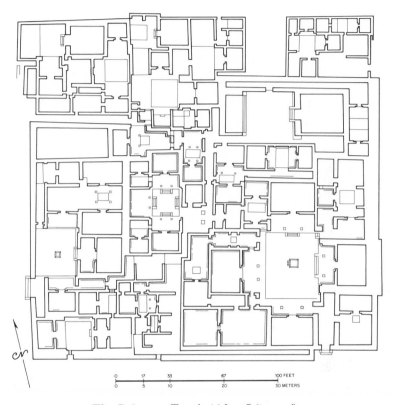

The Palace at Tetitla (After Séjourné)

The palaces were probably the residences of the priests and ruling families.

Very few tourists ever see the beautiful frescoed murals in the palaces of Tetitla and Atetelco. It takes the more intrepid traveler to discover that the great treasures at Teotihuacán

39

are just a few hundred yards beyond the main ceremonial center. It is necessary to use winding farm roads to reach these sites. The approach to Tetitla Palace runs parallel with corn fields and farmyards. Most of the walls throughout the palace have been reconstructed by archaeologists with porous basalt stone, the material of the original structure. This palace, like many of the others at Teotihuacán, covered a city block of the original city. On entering the Tetitla Palace, one is confronted with a mammoth maze of rooms. A series of patios throughout the palace must have served as areas for social gatherings at the time the palace was occupied. The patios also permitted light to penetrate into the surrounding rooms making this "maze" type of architecture functional. Narrow hallways between the various compounds of the palace permitted movement from one section to another. The whole palace has a perfect drainage system of underground canals and cisterns.

Before the palace was reconstructed, little of the ruins showed above ground level. However, many of the remaining walls below ground level, after 1,500 years of abandonment, still showed portions of their original murals. These murals were painted approximately A.D. 550. Archaeologists reconstructed the remaining walls up to a height that would give the visitor some feeling of how the palace originally looked. Corrugated modern ceilings are now placed over the rooms that still have murals to protect them from weathering.

All the rooms of the palace (there are reported to be fifty-six) are painted with different murals. The murals are highly formalized, with religious symbols and conventions in a style that is truly Teotihuacán. There is no indication here of a style imported from another culture. This type of formalized painting was to influence the tomb frescoes at Monte Albán, particularly in Tombs 104 and 105. Paintings at Tetitla were applied in the true fresco technique, that is, on wet plaster. Most of the colors came from mineral sources. As you enter the palace, a room in one of the patios to the right has a mural of a vulture holding a large conch shell. Sound scrolls issue from the vulture and the conch. The conch is one of the fer-

Detail of the coyote mural in the Tetitla Palace, Teotihuacán. Classic period.

tility symbols because of water association. Conch shells in murals are seen in many rooms of the palace. Throughout the whole ceremonial center of Teotihuacán the conch is represented in paintings and sculpture. On the Temple of Quetzalcoatl the conch, as well as other seashells, are a part of the sculptural decoration of the façade. In the mural at Tetitla the significance of the vulture and the conch is unknown. Other rooms in the palace structure contain murals of priests, trilobite hearts, and water symbols, coyotes, and birds. One room, referred to as the "red quetzal" room, has murals of a red bird symbolically represented in different ways on all of the four walls. Other murals represent Tláloc, the water deity, with large white-circled eyes, and the jaguar deity adorned with decorative flower-like symbols.

41

Detail of the red quetzal bird mural in the Tetitla Palace, Teotihuacán. Classic period.

In the farther end of the palace is a major courtyard show-ing several superimpositions. In fact, the many superimposi-tions throughout the palace indicate occupation for a long time. The courtyard is reached by descending a flight of steps. An *adoratorio* or small altar in the middle of this courtyard was also plastered and painted. The rooms opening into the court-yard all have interesting murals. The walls of the east room display a series of orange jaguars seated on stools. Temples are represented on the south wall in a style reminiscent of the contemporary painter, Miró. The most important fresco and the best preserved in this court is the one on the west wall. Here we see four representations of Tláloc, the Rain God,

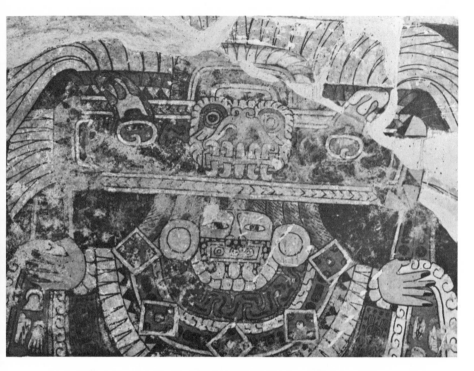

Detail of a mural depicting Tláloc, the rain deity. Tláloc is shown with long incisor teeth, nose piece, earrings, and an elaborate headdress of quetzal feathers. From his hands flow precious objects. Tetitla Palace, Teotihuacán. Classic period.

dressed in a great quetzal-feather headdress studded with white cotton pompoms. The front of the headdress is the beak of a bird. The mouth of Tláloc shows his long incisor teeth. His hair is braided, and large circular earplugs are placed in each ear. He also wears a rectangular-shaped nose piece. From his hanging hands flow drops of water and other precious symbols connected with this water deity. Amazingly, his fingernails are painted red. These four representations of Tláloc are no doubt priest impersonators dressed in the costume of Tláloc.

Murals in an adjoining room to this courtyard show a

43

Large sunken patio in the Palace of Atetelco, Teotihuacán. In the cen-
ter of the patio is an adoratorio *representing a small temple-pyramid.*
The patio and adoratorio *were painted in brilliant-colored frescos.*
Classic period.

priest on hands and knees, dressed in a jaguar skin with a
quetzal headdress, making his way toward a temple. His trail
is indicated by footprints. The great quetzal headdress used
here and the quetzal decorations on all things of a religious
nature throughout this palace suggest the importance of these
prestigious feathers. Even conches have feathered headdresses.
In another section of the palace is a mural of a fisherman
swimming underwater with a net in one hand while the other
hand is placing a shell into the net. These palace walls must
have been brilliant with murals before their destruction by
man and the weather.

44

A portion of the Patio Blanco now being reconstructed in the Palace of Atetelco, Teotihuacán. Classic period.

Just a few hundred yards from Tetitla is Atetelco, another important palace structure. One of the courtyards, the Patio Blanco (white patio), is now undergoing restoration and it is an extremely impressive complex. Each of the three porticoed structures facing the patio is completely painted in murals. The murals, different in each portico, are in tones of red, contrasting with the all-white patio and the white color of the porticoed chambers. In the north portico can be seen a priest or knight, dressed as Tláloc with spears and atlatl (spear thrower), hunting for a small marsh bird, the *chichieuilote,* which is represented in flight in each of the diamond-shaped repeat patterns making up the mural. The central wall of the north portico is painted with the eagle knight, again in a diamond-shaped repeat pattern.

45

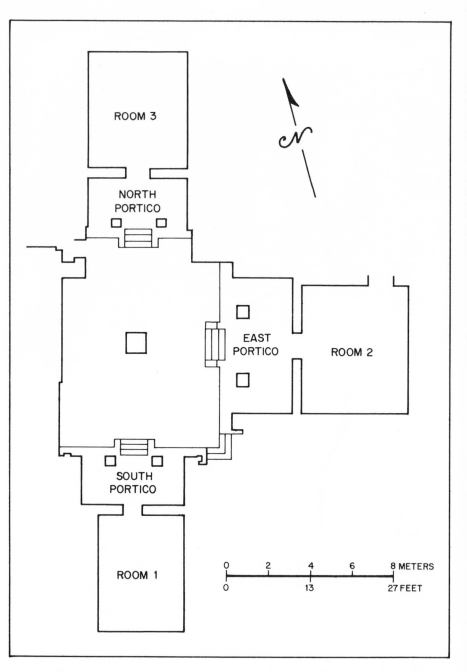

White Patio at Atetelco (Preliminary plans by Miller; completed by Halpin and Wilson)

The east portico of the Patio Blanco at Teotihuacán has been restored. In contrast to the white patio, all the murals are painted red. Classic period.

On the east porticoed chamber, the all-over diamond design is again filled with a representation of Tláloc holding a staff and spears. In the lower panels of this chamber is a representation of the coyote and jaguar. Border designs show a serpentine coyote and jaguar fashioned as an entwined snake form. Another interesting design encircles the door frame and represents a feathered serpent-coyote exhaling large sound scrolls. The south porticoed chamber is painted in a repeat design of the coyote knight with spears and atlatl. The large panels at the base of this mural are coyotes with shield symbols on their stomachs.

A coyote deity on the east portico of the Patio Blanco at Teotihuacán. A sound glyph and a trilobate heart issues from his mouth. His head has a crest of quetzal feathers. Classic period.

The muralist who painted the Patio Blanco complex was extremely consistent in the depiction of each of the murals. The major figure of the murals is a knight or priest in the center of each of the large diamond patterns. The diamond border design is made up of a decorative motif taken from parts of the knight's costume or other thematic material. Borders on the large dado panels at the base of the structures are handled in the same way.

Slowly this very important patio at Atetelco is being restored. The tedious task involves an artist's encrusting the original plaster from the mural on a recently plastered wall upon which the whole pattern of the mural has been outlined. After the original pieces are in place, the mural is reconstructed

A jaguar deity with a decorative net motif is located in the east portico of the Patio Blanco, Palace of Atetelco, Teotihuacán. Classic period.

as it originally appeared. So that the visitor can tell the original mural plaster from the reconstructed painting, the latter is painted in a darker red.

The Palace of the Jaguar and the Temple of the Feathered Shells are located under the Temple of Quetzalpapalotl adjacent to the Plaza of the Moon. This substructure was covered over at a later time by the Palace of Quetzalpapalotl. The Jaguar Palace is so named because of the many depictions of jaguars in rooms surrounding the open patios of the palace. The Palace of the Jaguar is approached by a stairway leading down to a large palace courtyard. The most important mural here is located in one of the north rooms of the courtyard. Its theme is a jaguar blowing a conch shell singing "a hymn to the sun." Both the jaguar and the conch have an ornate headdress of

49

Corner of the Jaguar's Palace, Teotihuacán. Construction shows the use of wooden lintels and dressed stone. The beads of miniature pebbles in the cement indicate reconstruction by the archaeologists.

quetzal feathers. Above the jaguar is a border design representing Tláloc, alternating with the "year sign." An adjacent room of this palace has a series of blue painted jaguars in a linear design—quite a remarkable representation by the artist.

A narrow passageway from the palace courtyard leads to the Temple of the Feathered Conch. This handsome façade of the temple is decorated with one of the finest low-relief carvings at Teotihuacán. The carvings of plumed conches and a four-petaled flower motif are on vertical shafts of stone that are a part of the temple façade. The platform to this temple has a *tablero* decorated with a fresco painting of green parrot-like birds with drops of water exuding from their yellow beaks. The molding of the *tablero* has circle decorations representing "jade" or "precious"—terms that denote significance. This structure is believed to have been constructed some time between the second and third century.

Above the Temple of the Jaguar is the Palace of Quetzalpapalotl (Palace of the Plumed Butterfly). In order to create a platform for the erection of the Palace of Quetzalpapalotl,

Blue and red jaguars decorate the walls of the dado in the Palace of the Jaguar, Teotihuacán. Classic period.

Patio of the Palace of Quetzalpapalotl, Teotihuacán. Merlons of stone, plastered and painted, decorate the roof to this palace courtyard. Classic period.

the Temple of the Jaguars was partially destroyed and filled in with rubble. The restoration of the Palace of Quetzalpapalotl was faithfully carried out so that today we are able to see this palace, and below it the Temple of the Jaguar. The courtyard to the Palace of Quetzalpapalotl is a creation of the talents of the architects and sculptors during the latter days (possibly seventh century) of the Classic era for Teotihuacán. The roof of the courtyard, open to the sky, is decorated with large red-painted stone merlons, representing the "year sign."

Supporting the roof of the patio are square columns carved in low relief with representations of butterflies and parrots. These columns were once covered with a fine coating of lime plaster and painted. Stone insertions for the eyes of the birds and butterflies were of obsidian stone, some of which remain today. Other symbols on these pillars are taken from conch shells, feathers, and the circle for "precious." Very little remains of the murals around the porticoed chambers although there is some indication of a stepped fret motif to suggest the style of decoration.

The three rooms that open into this courtyard have the greatest room span so far known in Mesoamerica. There are no supporting beams and the rooms are approximately twenty-six feet square. The roof was at one time timbered and then plastered and painted.

Murals in the palace structure of Tepantitla are more popularly known than those of Tetitla or Atetelco because of the subject matter. The ruins of the palace of Tepantitla are located a short distance east of the Pyramid of the Sun. This structure was another of the many palaces that surrounded the main ceremonial area, and it may have been a residence for the priestly class. There are indications of murals in many of the rooms. However, the porticoed chamber with the sunken patio has the two most interesting murals. On the top part of one wall are two dramatic murals of the Rain God, Tláloc, dominating two interesting scenes below. One is that of a ball game in action. Even the goal or marker of the ball court is visible. The other scene is that of the Paradise of the Rain

*Supporting columns for the portico in the Palace of Quetzalpapalotl
are carved in low relief using a bird and butterfly motif. Teotihuacán.
Classic period.*

Detail of a column in the Palace of Quetzalpapalotl. Obsidian stones for the eyes are still encrusted in some of the reliefs. These reliefs were given a thin coat of lime, and then painted in brilliant colors. Teotihuacán. Classic period.

Portion of the "ball game" mural at Tepantitla Palace, Teotihuacán. Toward the top of the mural can be seen the ball-court marker. Players carry clubs used during the games. Reconstructed mural in the Museum of Anthropology, Mexico City.

God. In this scene we see Tláloc presiding over the heavenly joys of persons who are enjoying their newfound paradise. In a highly animated style persons are depicted chasing animals, eating fruits of the land, and enjoying the pleasures of fish from the river which is flowing or springing from the nearby mountain. The scene is a great one. Since the painting is in bad condition, even as restored, it can be better appreciated if seen first in its entirety at the Museo Nacional de Antropología e Historia in Mexico City.

There are many other murals at Teotihuacán scattered over a wide area. A splendid mural of an orange jaguar can be seen on a *tablero* of one of the temple platforms along the Pathway of the Dead. In this same area there is a unique mural

Detail of mural in the Tepantitla Palace, Teotihuacán. Tláloc, the rain deity, is distributing seeds from his hand. Reconstructed mural in the Museum of Anthropology, Mexico City. Classic period.

of the Mythological Animals that still has to be restored and is not open to the public. The Temple of Agriculture also contained murals which unfortunately have deteriorated because they were painted on unbaked clay. However, good copies of these exist in the museum in Mexico City.

Mural painting, during the Classic period, reached a great florescence, not only here at Teotihuacán but also at Monte Albán and in the Maya area. If we are to judge from the Bonampak murals, the Maya style of fresco painting was realistic, recording the happenings of contemporary life. In contrast, that of Monte Albán and Teotihuacán was formalized, depicting the many deities and other religious conventions. It is fortunate that enough frescoes are extant to give us a good representation of Classic mural painting. Because of the perish-

56

Upper panel to the Paradise of the Rain God mural, Tepantitla, Teotihuacán. Tláloc is shown reigning over the paradise below. His great crown, filled with water symbols, birds, and flowers, is especially imposing. Reconstructed mural in the Museum of Anthropology, Mexico City. Classic period.

able nature of fresco painting, it seems amazing that any have withstood the destructive forces of man and nature. However, at Teotihuacán are over forty structures that have been uncovered which have murals on the lower parts of the walls. Among these are over three hundred different designs. The exteriors of all buildings were at one time painted with murals, suggesting there may have been some ten thousand murals in the city. This principal art form was not reserved for tombs as at Monte Albán, but was used on shrines, temples, palaces, and lesser habitations. Secular and religious ceremonies were greatly enhanced by the color and the brilliancy of the murals and the pageantry that accompanied them.

57

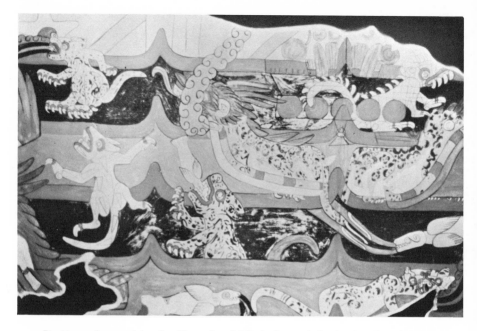

Portion of mural in the Temple of Mythological Animals, Teotihuacán. Reconstructed mural in the Museum of Anthropology, Mexico City. Classic period.

Cholula

A looming glow in the peach-colored sky is reflected in the shimmering pools of water along the highway leading to Cholula. The air is crisp and cold. The forbidding mountains in the distant landscape are pierced by two snow-capped peaks glowing in the morning light. Famed in legends and myths and worshiped for eternity, are Popocatépetl and Iztaccihuatl more popularly known as "Smoky Mountain" and "Sleeping Lady." From here the modest descent is gradual into the rich, farm country approaching Cholula. Noises of children from the clustered compounds of village houses have the peculiar quality that such sounds take on when heard through the splashing water of honking cars and buses. Brilliant tiled domes of Cholula's many churches signify the approaching city. The ancient city of Cholula is just one of the archaeological reminders of man and his presence in the Valley of Mexico from the earliest of times.

A few years ago the pyramid of Cholula looked like any other of the many natural high hills jutting out of these vast plains, most of which were at one time active volcanic cones. When the Spaniards built their city around this pyramid, they crowned the top of this great hill with a church, now known as the Church of *Nuestra Señora de los Remedios*. The city of Cholula was a very important shrine area for the Indians before the Spanish Conquest. At that time there was reported to have been over two hundred temples crowning the many hills in the distant landscape. All these "pagan" temples were destroyed by the conquerors. It is only a miracle that the great pyramid of Cholula and its surrounding structures were buried far beneath the ground, unknown to any but the Indians. The Spaniards continued to construct their own houses of worship, and within a few years the city was said to have had 364 additional churches. At the time of the Spanish Conquest the city and its suburbs had approximately 40,000 houses, indicating a dense urban center. Only the city of Tenochtitlán was larger. Today the population of the city is a scant 15,000 to 20,000 and most of the churches are slowly disintegrating, adding to the pile of archaeological data for future historians.

Recent excavations at the great pyramid now reveal the tremendous size of the structure and the complexity of the vast building programs undertaken over the centuries. The pyramid is the largest in volume of any in the Americas and larger than the more famous Egyptian pyramid of Cheops. The base is 1,400 feet on each side and covers approximately 46 acres. The approximate height is 198 feet. The actual height before the temple on its peak was destroyed might have been 20 or 30 feet more. At a lower level than the temple were the quarters for the priests. Burials have been found here as well. This whole area of ruins was obliterated when the Spaniards constructed the church on the summit of the pyramid.

The Great Plaza and pyramid at Cholula. A Spanish church was built on top of the pyramid in colonial times. Recent excavation is seen in the foreground.

This great pyramid must have compared favorably with the pyramids of the Sun and Moon at Teotihuacán, its contemporaries. When Teotihuacán was abandoned in the seventh century, Cholula became the focal point of culture in the Valley of Mexico.

Excavations started at Cholula in 1931 under the direction of José Reygadas Vertis and continued under Ignacio Marquína. Over four miles of tunnels were made through the pyramid in order to establish its chronology and the types of structures in use at various times and to discover burials and caches that might indicate the cultural development. Today the tunnels are electrified so that travelers can enter and study the various building sequences.

Cholula was occupied in Late Preclassic times (400–100

B.C.), and the earliest platforms are of mud and stone. From this time on, there were at least six major superimpositions. The temple pyramid complex was believed to have been dedicated to Quetzelcoatl, an important god at Teotihuacán and later with the Toltecs and Aztecs. Monumental construction started in the second century and continued until the end of the eighth century when the ceremonial center reached a hiatus. During this time Cholula was highly influenced by that great classic city, Teotihuacán, just one hundred miles to the north. This is especially noted in the architecture in which the *talud-tablero* type decoration for platforms was widely used. Teotihuacán influence is also apparent in the murals, ceramics, and deities depicted. Cholula was also to come under the influence of the Gulf Coast city of El Tajín, believed to have been the capital of the Classic Veracruz civilization. This influence is especially noted in the monumental sculpture. Evidently a very important city, not only for a great variety of crafts but also as a trade center, Cholula exchanged merchandise with Monte Albán, Xochicalco, and many other noted cities both in the highlands and along the Gulf Coast. Merchants and professional craftsmen were probably in organized guilds, differing in status according to their specialization.

Most of the construction at Cholula was of adobe, faced with small stones, and then given a heavy coating of plaster or clay. This was then painted. On walking through the tunnels in the interior of the pyramid, one notices a Teotihuacán-like *tablero* painted in red, yellow, and black with a series of large insects, possibly grasshoppers. These tunnels also reveal the construction of the various superimpositions, and a view of the major staircase of cut stone that leads to the top of the pyramid. The top part of the staircase has not been excavated. The tunnel can be entered on the north side of the pyramid near the small museum. It is sometimes possible to exit on the east side of the pyramid when that portion of the tunnel is open to the public.

It is difficult to visualize that within the interior of this great man-made hill of adobe is a pyramid (Pyramid C) larger

61

than the Pyramid of the Moon at Teotihuacán. Pyramid C is 150 feet high. The present pyramid was constructed over this great shell. Pyramids A and B, in the very interior, are of a much earlier date, possibly built as early as the first or second century A.D.

In the recent excavations on the exterior base of the pyramid it was necessary to remove tons of earth that had accumulated over the centuries. This accumulation was as deep as thirty to thirty-five feet. This earth protected the pyramid platforms over the years, and, when excavated, they were in fair condition. However, the structures on the platforms had long since perished, and this tremendous pressure of tons of earth was destructive to the monuments and many of the structures and foundations. Excavations revealed a series of large plazas and courtyards surrounded by platforms, indicating a ceremonial center of considerable size. The many superimpositions surrounding this plaza make the area one of the most complex to study. Archaeologists have left great series of excavated platforms and stairways exposed so that one may see the immense building activities over the centuries. The labor force needed to amass the construction materials for such an under-

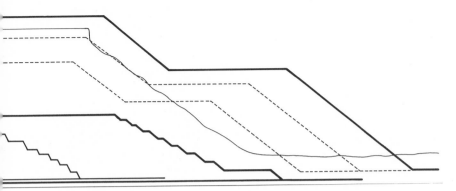

Cholula Pyramid, Showing Superimpositions (After I. Marquina)

taking could only have come from a populace who were controlled by an elite theocratic group that had the power to harness labor forces of thousands of people.

Excavations on the south side of the pyramid give proof to the enormity of the Cholula project. The Great Plaza, also called *Patio de los Altares,* is over an acre in size and was designed as the approach to the grand staircase for the pyramid. Surrounding this Great Plaza is a series of structures, burial chambers, platforms, and monuments. In its time the approach must have been a splendid one and impressive enough to equal the ceremonial centers of other great cities of that era. The major part of the construction on the south side of the pyramid was begun in the second and third centuries. Additions were made and older sections covered over in the years that followed.

The remains of many murals can be seen on the various structures surrounding the plaza. Most of these murals are in bold geometric designs interspersed with starlike patterns. A similar style of decoration is seen on some structures at Teotihuacán. The most spectacular mural revealed to date at Cholula is on the west side of the Great Plaza, located in an

Recent excavations on the south side of the pyramid at Cholula reveal the many superimpositions of earlier structures built between the second and seventh centuries A.D.

interior structure built between the second and third centuries. The mural depicts a ceremonial drinking scene that might have taken place at the time of harvest. The participants in the scene are all men except for two old, wrinkled women, and they are seated on a platform draped in a fabric. A dog and a flying bee also can be seen. The ceremony is well under way as the participants have extended stomachs from the liquor. Their dress is scanty. Mostly nude, the figures have waistbands and adornments for the neck and ears. Some of the men wear ceremonial masks. In a scale that is life size, this magnificent mural is over 150 feet long and is painted in shades of red, ochre, and blue. The freedom in the style of painting is rarely encountered in Mesoamerica. Here the artist has used cryptic brush strokes with free-flowing curves that outline very real-

Quadrilateral fret motifs decorate the walls of the Great Plaza at Cholula. Stairways are constructed diagonally to the rectangular symmetry of the plaza.

istically the human figures drinking their liquor. It is a scene of great joy and abandonment. Only in the Tepantitla palace structure at Teotihuacán is there such freedom of style in a mural. There, in the mural depicting the Paradise of the Rain God, Tláloc, a carefree style is used for the heavenly joys of the animated people in a glorious paradise scene. However, the Paradise of the Rain God at Teotihuacán is believed to have been painted a century or two later than the famous drinking scene at Cholula.

The shapes of the pottery in the Cholula mural and those pieces found within the structure are in the style of Teotihuacán II, contemporary with Cholula II, dating from the second to the third century. Although damaged by water seepage in many places, the mural is still in a fairly good state

65

Head carved from a basalt boulder discovered during excavation of the Great Plaza, Cholula.

of repair. Further restoration of the mural was carefully undertaken by the Instituto Nacional de Antropologia e Historia.

Surrounding the Great Plaza are platforms of cut stone decorated with quadrilateral fret motifs. In the corners of the plaza are stairways constructed diagonally to this rectangular symmetry. Earlier superimpositions excavated here show that the diagonal stairway must have been employed over a long period of time. It is unique to Cholula.

A number of large stone monuments are located in the Great Plaza. Three of these that now can be seen in the northwest corner are crudely carved, indicating that they may be either provincial imports or heirloom sculptures carved at an earlier time than the plaza construction. They could be sculptures from Preclassic time. They may have been placed here because of their importance or brought into the plaza as cult objects at a later date. Indication of plaster on the stone suggests that they were originally painted.

The three most important stone monuments at Cholula are singularly located on the north, east, and west sides of the plaza. They are all carved in a similar style to Classic Veracruz. Broken in fragments when found, the monuments are repaired and re-erected in their original positions. Monument 1 is a handsomely carved rectangular-shaped stone approximately twelve feet high, which rests on a large, rectangular stone slab, and is located on the east side of the plaza. A double-outlined interlocking scroll design, carved in low relief, forms a border to the monument. Since the central section of the monument is left uncarved, it is quite possible a sculpture of one of the deities or an offering may have been placed in front of the plain panel. The top of the monument is missing.

Monument 3 is placed in front of the stairway on the north side of the plaza. Again, the stone is carved in the same fine style as Monument 1. On the east side of the Great Plaza is Altar 2, another large rectangular stone slab lying horizontally. At one time there may have been a vertical monument placed here similar to Monument 1. However, in excavating the area, no such monument was found. Altar 2 is a single stone weighing approximately ten tons. It is distinctive in that the vertical edge is carved in an entwined serpent motif. Particles of plaster on the stone indicate that the sculpture was at one time plastered and painted. Again, the style is highly reminiscent of Classic Veracruz. It is quite possible that the architects, sculptors, and craftsmen may have been visiting itinerants at each other's cities from time to time, where an exchange of ideas and artifacts was possible. Cholula certainly exerted an enormous influence in the Valley of Mexico throughout its history.

On excavating the south side of the Great Plaza, archaeologists discovered an Aztec tomb that was constructed here

Monument 3 located at the north end of the Great Plaza, Cholula. An interlocking scroll, carved in low relief, forms a border to the monument. Classic period.

Altar 2 on the east side of the Great Plaza, Cholula. This monolithic stone slab has a low relief carving of two entwined serpents. Classic period.

many centuries after the abandonment of this area by the original inhabitants. The large tomb and its contents have been left on display for the visitor to study.

On the west side of the Cholula pyramid another magnificently carved platform has been reconstructed. Here, again, the influence of Teotihuacán is seen in the use of the *talud* and *tablero*. The carved design within the *tablero* is a braid or basket-weave motif that is not known to be used in this way anywhere else. Water drains on this structure are clearly placed so as not to interfere with the vertical pattern on the platform cornices.

Two important sculptures were found in the area of this latter platform. One, a stylized serpent that may have been

69

Restored platform on the west side of the great pyramid at Cholula. The tablero *is decorated in a braid design. Vertical water drains can be seen going over the* talud *and under the* tablero. *Classic period.*

part of a balustrade, was removed from the site. The other is an extremely large vertical shaft of stone, slightly irregular in shape, showing very little carving. In the center of the stone a rectangular opening has been carved. The purpose of the monument is unknown, but it must have had some religious significance to this particular ceremonial center. The design is abstract enough to have been made by one of the modern sculptors of our time.

Only a fraction of the Cholula area has been excavated. Most of its history is still clouded in mystery. We know the area was occupied from Middle Preclassic times to the present day. There is little known of the people who inhabited the area, their language, or the extent of their political control during the centuries that marked the Classic period when the

Stylized serpent head found during excavation of the west side of the great pyramid at Cholula.

pyramid complex was constructed. The dominance of Teotihuacán over Cholula and other Classic cities in the Valley of Mexico cannot be dismissed lightly. Interrelationships between the cities, their political organization, and the degree of autonomous rule are research tasks still to be undertaken. It seems apparent that with the lack of fortifications at Cholula as well as at other earlier Classic sites and with their *idée fixé* in regard to gods of harvest, rain, and other peaceful deities, Cholula may have been the last of the cultural areas that was dominated by priestly rulers. By Postclassic times, a new-styled military order was to change the nature of the political organization throughout Mesoamerica.

During the Postclassic period a new style of pottery evolved in the Cholula-Puebla area that was painted in fret and other

71

bold geometric designs in which polychrome was used. This particular style of pottery is referred to as Mixteca, one of the trade pieces found in abundance at Tula. Plumbate pottery has also been found at Cholula, indicating trade as far south as Guatemala. Plumbate is believed not to have reached the region before the twelfth century. Mixteca codices and the Spanish chronicles indicate that Cholula was a meeting place for merchants and pilgrims from all over Mexico and Central America, creating a cosmopolitan city that had a great cultural impact on other cultures in Mesoamerica as far south as Tulum in Quintana Roo and Santa Rita in British Honduras, and locations in Honduras, El Salvador, and Nicaragua. The east coast sites of Zempoala, Isla de Sacrificios, and Cerro de las Mesas were also influenced by this pervasive style from the Puebla-Cholula area.

Tula

During the dry season, the countryside en route to Tula is a faded beige, barren, and seemingly lifeless. Distant mountains on a hazy horizon are in a shroud of mauve light from the early morning sun. Geometric patches of lush green gardens are spotted in some of the valleys where irrigation has been possible from mountain streams. Before the Spanish Conquest, an irrigation system had been used by the Indians of this region for a thousand years. With the draining of Lake Texcoco by the Spaniards, a great lake that supplied the water needs for much of this countryside, the land soon yielded little produce for the populace. At this same time many irrigation projects had to be abandoned. Today it is hard to visualize this valley as one that produced enough food to maintain great

Facing page: *Unusual stone sculpture, abstract in design, discovered in excavating the west side of the pyramid at Cholula.*

populations for two mighty pre-Conquest empires, that of the Toltecs and the Aztecs.

Myths and legends are of little help in knowing the beginnings of the ascending Toltec strength in this area. As early as Late Classic times, possibly as early as the eighth century, bands of Chichimec tribal peoples, speaking the Nahuatl language, moved into the various valleys of this highland region. According to legend, they came from the northwest area of Mexico and were without any culture. With the gradual abandonment of Teotihuacán and the eclipse of Cholula, some time between the sixth and eighth centuries, the Toltec people gradually assimilated the culture of these two great political centers and started on a tenacious conquest program. For a time they occupied the Teotihuacán site, and no doubt some of the mounds not excavated to date may prove to be Toltec. By the beginning of the ninth century they were well established in several centers in the valley. Their influence was felt at Cholula and Xochicalco, and one of their early cities was Tenayuca. The degree of their control in these areas is difficult to establish. During this same time, Mixtec Indians were also gathering strength for control of much of this same territory. Certainly by the end of the tenth century the Toltecs had established their capital at Tula. The rule from this city lasted a little over two hundred years, when Tula was burned and shortly thereafter abandoned. Aztec warriors sacked the city in 1156, carrying off much of the sculpture and construction materials.

Although this short-lived empire was based on a culture that in the main was eclectic, its influence was felt as far east as the Veracruz coast and as far south as Yucatán. There is good reason to believe that the Toltecs had filtered into that area in Late Classic times (A.D. 600–900). Other Toltec peoples may have been the intrusive groups that reached the Pasión River area of the Petén during this same time. No doubt the demand for such luxury items as cocoa, feathers, and cotton were factors in the Toltec positioning for control

74

in areas far from their homeland. In the eleventh century they established their second capital city at Chichén Itzá in Yucatán. Two centuries later the Toltecs were no longer an empire, and their capital cities were abandoned for reasons unaccounted for to the present day.

According to legend the Toltecs were first ruled by the terrifying conqueror, Mixcoatl or "Cloud Serpent." His rule was followed by his son Ce Acatl Topiltzin, "Our Lord One Reed," who adopted the name Quetzalcoatl, a deity well known at Teotihuacán in Classic time. He expanded the Toltec supremacy in the valley and established a capital at Tula. It is believed a dual political organization may have been used at Tula in which secular and religious responsibilities were separated. Because of Topiltzin's difficulties in leading his people, his overindulgence in liquor and women, and his refusal to offer no more than birds, snakes, and butterflies for sacrifices to the gods, he became unpopular, and he left the rule of Tula to his contender, Huemac, and started on a program of conquest by going to Yucatán with some of his followers, leaving a legend that at some time he would return to rule again. At Chichén Itzá, the location of a large abandoned Classic Maya city, he established a capital, altering the existing Maya architecture for his own needs, and then had his architects, with the aid of Maya craftsmen, create new structures that were based in part on the model city of Tula.

Archaeologists have been excavating in the Tula site ever since findings appeared in the publication *Les Anciennes Villes du Nouveau Monde* in 1888. Further investigations were made by Jiménez Moreno in 1938. More recent excavation and restoration, under the direction of Jorge Acosta, has been undertaken by the Instituto Nacional de Antropologia e Historia. Today there is enough of the ceremonial center restored for us to appreciate how impressive this capital city once must have been and how it may have functioned. The Great Plaza at Tula covers several acres, and must have been the ceremonial center for military extravaganzas, religious celebrations, festivals, pa-

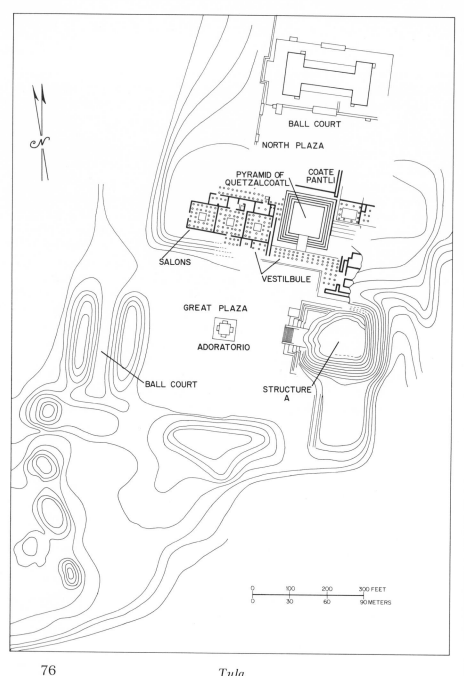

BALL COURT

NORTH PLAZA

PYRAMID OF QUETZALCOATL

COATE PANTLI

SALONS

VESTILBULE

GREAT PLAZA

ADORATORIO

BALL COURT

STRUCTURE A

0   100   200   300 FEET
0   30   60   90 METERS

Tula

General view of the Toltec ceremonial center at Tula. Pyramid of Quetzalcoatl in the distance and the Great Plaza in the foreground now covered with grass. Ceremonial platform to the left, and Building C to the right. Postclassic.

rades, and performances of drama and music. In the center of the plaza is a ceremonial platform very similar to platforms at Teotihuacán, having a stairway on all four sides and employing the *talud-tablero* style of architecture. Désiré Charnay excavated here and misunderstood the nature of the mound. This made the reconstruction difficult and questionable. Surrounding the plaza are a group of other structures, little of which remain today. The principle pyramid (Building C) to the east of the plaza has not been excavated. The facing stones were removed many centuries ago, and today the pyramid is in poor repair, looking like a mound of earth with some indication of a stairway. To the left of the stairway is a small shrine built by the Aztecs some centuries later.

To the west of the Great Plaza are additional platforms and a ball court which has at least two superimpositions,

Building C, Tula. This was the principal pyramid at Tula. The facing stones of the pyramid and the superstructure have vanished over the years. Postclassic.

and it has been partially restored. This ball court is the largest found so far on the Mexican plateau, having a length well over 350 feet. Several other ball courts at Tula indicate the importance of the game. The longest ball court in Mesoamerica is at Chichén Itzá. It is 450 feet in length and was also constructed by the Toltecs.

The buildings at Tula were constructed with riverbed stones and rubble mixed with cement. This masonry was faced with dressed stone, given a thick plaster coating, and then painted. This type of construction can be seen at the ball court and the Great Vestibule to the north of the plaza. Great

Partial columns, reconstructed, are all that remain of the Great Vestibule at Tula. The Pyramid of Quetzalcoatl is just behind this colonnade. Postclassic.

numbers of columns were used for this dramatic vestibule. A colonnaded arcade, creating an avenue of square columns, ran parallel to the north and east side of the Great Plaza, forming the Great Vestibule. These columns at one time supported a roof, but today only the partially reconstructed columns remain. From the Great Vestibule area the elite of the time could watch the ceremonies in the Great Plaza and at the same time be protected from the heat of the midday sun. At one time a bench ran the total length of the vestibule, but only a portion of it remains today. The bench was decorated with a series of warriors carved in low relief and painted in bright colors.

Behind this avenue of ninety-seven columns that formed

A remaining portion of the bench that at one time ran the length of the Great Vestibule, Tula. Relief carving on the lower portion of the bench is a series of warriors. A serpent design is carved on the top part of the bench. Postclassic.

the Great Vestibule are three porticoed salons with sunken, open patios. Two of these salons have circular columns that supported the roof while the third salon has square columns. It is quite possible that this area could have been the palace for the ruler of Tula. However, these salons were more apt to have been the judicial or council halls or the administrative seat since there are daises and benches located around the walls. Square depressions in the floor were for fireboxes. There are two chacmools in the central salon, one of them broken. Chacmools are sculptured stone figures reclining on their backs. On their stomachs is a depression where offerings may have been placed or where an eternal flame could be seen. The figure of the chacmool is clothed in a short loin cloth. Ornamentation consists of a short knife tied to his upper left arm,

80

The remainder of columns that at one time supported three porticoed salons that may have been part of the palace at Tula. Postclassic.

a nose plug, square earplugs, bracelets, and a headdress. Chacmools were a favorite subject for sculpture both at Tula and at Chichén Itzá.

The most important structure at Tula is the Temple of Quetzalcoatl (Structure B). It is easily recognized by the monumental sculptured basalt columns on the top platform. When archaeologists excavated this mound, the columns were discovered, having been buried under the pyramid for many centuries. This burial must have taken place before the Aztecs came into their ascendency. Recently the columns have been restored to the top of the platform.

Divided into five platforms and at one time completely faced with large panels of carved stone, the Pyramid of Quetzalcoatl is an extremely compelling, unique structure. Fortunately the pyramid was partially buried by the shifting soil

A Toltec chacmool of basalt located in a courtyard of one of the salons at Tula. Postclassic.

over the many centuries, and only those panels exposed above the ground level were taken either by vandals, the Spaniards, or the Aztecs to be used for their own construction purposes at other locations. Now that the pyramid is cleared of this earth fill, we can see the exposed, carved stone slabs in the lower east side. Panels on the *tablero* as well as the cornice above it are carved in low relief. The cornice decoration is a repetitive pattern of a coyote and a jaguar alternating across the length of the side of the building. The *tablero* section of the pyramid depicts what may have represented the god Venus or Quetzalcoatl held in the mouth of a feathered serpent. Alternating with this design are two stylized eagles eating a trifoil-shaped heart. These designs were to appear again in faraway Yucatán when the Toltecs built their second empire city at Chichén Itzá. With the aid of the great Maya craftsmen, sculp-

82

Carved panels on the exterior surface of the Pyramid of Quetzalcoatl at Tula.

ture in low relief at the latter site was to reach a much loftier level than at Tula.

The approach to the Temple of Quetzalcoatl is by a short but steep stairway. At one time the stairs were bordered by a balustrade. The two-room temple on top of the platform has long since disappeared as well as the feathered serpent columns that supported the lintel at its entrance. The great columns that supported the wood-beamed roof have now been restored to their original positions. The first four columns that supported the roof of the first chamber are carved in a heroic, theatrical, awe-inspiring manner. These formal columns, nearly fifteen feet high, are all carved alike. Here is Quetzalcoatl in the guise of Venus, the evening star. This guise is taken from a legend in which Quetzalcoatl, en route to Yucatán, met his death and was buried on a funeral pyre

Detail of the carved panels on the Pyramid of Quetzalcoatl, Tula. The tablero *is decorated with coyotes, jaguars, and eagles eating hearts. Postclassic.*

at sea. The flame of the pyre then became the evening star. In these sculptures is a warrior, standing stiffly erect and crowned with a headdress having a band of stars from which protrude a circle of vertical feathers. Depressions for the eyes and mouth suggest an inlay of obsidian or bone may have been used. The warrior's dress is a triangular-shaped, fringed skirt tied at the back with a large circular disc, representing the sun, which acts as a clasp or button for the skimpy skirt. The warrior's buttocks are bare. A great breastplate representing a butterfly typifies the "warrior"-type pendant worn by the Toltec. A string of beads is around his neck and square ear ornaments decorate his head. In his hands are a spear and spear thrower, the *atlatl.* Attached to his upper arm is a short

Heroic sculptures of warriors supported the roof of the Temple of Quetzalcoatl, Tula. Postclassic.

spear blade pointing skyward. Sandals and bracelets are adorned with serpent motifs.

The column on the far left is a stone replica of the original, which is now in the Museum of Anthropology in Mexico City. Part of the right column was not recovered during excavation and it also has been duplicated. These great stone columns of Quetzalcoatl are not monoliths but are cut in sections and tenoned together. In this way the stones could more easily be moved from the quarry to the ceremonial center before the carving was started. Behind the columns are four additional square columns that supported the roof of the second chamber of this temple. The relief on these is of the same warrior sub-

*Warrior columns were carved in sections and tennoned together.
Temple of Quetzalcoatl, Tula. Postclassic.*

Part of the Coatepantli wall running to the north of the Temple of Quetzalcoatl, Tula. Postclassic.

ject, Quetzalcoatl, and they are also doweled in sections. Long since disappeared, the flat roof of this temple was supported by wooden beams, plastered over and painted. Merlons encircled the top of the temple, creating an impressive, fanciful roof crest.

To the north, and parallel to the back of the Pyramid of Quetzalcoatl, is a high wall 130 feet long known as the Coatepantli. This wall separated the area of the ceremonial activities from what is believed to have been the residential area. The Coatepantli also continued along the sides of the pyramid. Covering the wall is a frieze, in low relief, of serpents devouring the skeletal bones of a man. Borders above and below this frieze are in a geometric pattern that is reminiscent of the step-and-fret designs used by the Mixtecs in their pottery designs and in their place at Mitla and Yagul. The Coatepantli

87

Detail of the Coatepantli wall, Tula. Borders of stepped fret designs. Central panel of serpents devouring men. The wall merlons are stylized conch shells in cross section.

is crowned with a crest of conchlike seashells in cross-section as merlons, and the whole wall was painted in brilliant colors with some indication of the color remaining today. This free-standing wall was decorated in a similar manner on both sides.

To the north of the plaza that separates the Coatepantli from the residential area is another restored ball court. At one time this ball court was faced with cut stones similar to those on the Temple of Quetzalcoatl, but they are believed to have been removed by the Aztecs when the city was plundered. The ball court is quite similar to the one at Xochicalco, and indeed it may have been the model. However, it is not quite as large (120 feet long) as that at Xochicalco. Although stone rings are not on the vertical playing walls of the Tula court

Ball court, Tula. Ball rings of stone were inserted into the side walls for scoring in the game. Postclassic.

today, there is some indication that they were there at one time. Both end walls of the court have stairways, and niches are placed in these walls as well. Other courts with niches are at Monte Albán, courts built at a much earlier time by the Zapotecs. These niches may have been for deities associated with the ball game or the playing teams. They could also have been designed for containers used for ablutions before or after the game. The plastered floor was well drained and the drainage system, after a thousand years, still works today.

Approximately one mile north of the main ceremonial center along a rough dirt road is a single structure called El Corral. The circular part of the structure is earlier than its two side wings, and it may have been a temple to the Wind God, Ehécatl. A later superimposition was added on both sides of the structure, creating two rectangular wings. The stairway, now in bad repair, was the approach to the circular central structure. The temple buildings that crowned these high platforms have long since disappeared. The platforms, however, are in good condition, and the original plaster can be seen.

89

El Corral, Tula. A circular structure with rectangular wings that may have been dedicated to the Wind God, Ehécatl. Postclassic.

To one side of this structure a small altar is visible that still shows the remains of a low relief consisting of skulls and crossbones and a series of standing warriors.

Between El Corral and the main ceremonial center and far beyond this area are large clusters of habitation sites. Many surface remains and mounds are visible. In this area the city has no particular orientation or integrated plan that seems apparent. No scientific study has been undertaken on the extent of the total population or the variations in population density.

Facing page: *Atlantean figure with original paint. Figures of this type were used to support tables, seats, and sometimes lintels of doorways. Tula Museum. Postclassic.*

90

Approximately four miles southeast of the ceremonial center of Tula is a hill area called Cielito. Recent excavations indicate the erection of Toltec structures during its early history and a later building program during the Aztec occupation. It is quite possible that this was the location of the palace occupied by Don Pedro Moctezuma, son of the last ruler of the Aztec, who was the cacique of Tula. Earlier, Don Pedro had been converted to Christianity and studied at the College of Tlatelolco in Mexico City.

Adjacent to the ruins at Tula is a small museum. Here can be seen Atlantean figures, incense burners, chacmools, ceramics, and other artifacts that are Toltec. Also included in the collection are a few Aztec ceramics that were found in the area and are of a late date. Some trade items from other regions of Mesoamerica found during excavation are also in the museum. Not only did the conquests of the Toltecs bring much foreign produce to the area, but the Toltecs picked up many ideas in architecture and in the lesser arts that are distinct trademarks of other cultures. Such centers as Monte Albán, Mitla, Cholula, Xochicalco, Teotihuacán, and El Tajín were all to be part of the eclecticism that was reflected in the empire city of Tula.

Although the architecture and art forms had a rustic vitality that was expressive, the city for the most part was built to impress the populace or foreign visitors. The construction was poor, and the murals were often painted on adobe rather than plaster, suggesting a technical poverty on the part of the craftsmen. The art forms seem stilted, unimaginative in their variety, crude in technique, and often poorly conceived. This is in marked contrast to Chichén Itzá, the second empire city of the Toltec. At Chichén Itzá, with the aid of Maya craftsmen, the Toltecs created an art style that is beautifully conceived, shows great technical facility, and has an elegance not known at Tula.

It was at Tula, however, that many of the original ideas for the art forms of the Toltecs were created. It was here that unique caryatid warriors were conceived as columns for the most important building. Both seated and standing carved stone standard bearers became part of the architectural sculpture. And at Tula Atlantean figures in great numbers were used to hold up benches and altars and became another popular sculptural form that was placed in many of the rooms. The lapidary work in mosaic stones produced some of the greatest masks, shields, and other art forms in Postclassic times. Not only was Tula to set the style for the newly created city of Chichén Itzá, but later the Aztecs were to take over this architectural and sculptural heritage and incorporate it in their construction of the city of Tenochtitlán on Lake Texcoco.

Tenayuca and Santa Cecilia

A drive through one of the economically poorer sections on the outskirts of Mexico City will lead to the pyramids of Tenayuca and Santa Cecilia. There is no more interesting way to see the daily life of Mexico's populace. Along the narrow walled streets are Indians and mestizos carrying pails of milk, platters of white cheese, and newly woven fabrics tied inside great sacks to tumplines pulled tightly around countrymen's foreheads. Everyone has a task to perform that will add to the meager living, even to the smallest child. Many of the day's activities center around the local markets, where all villagers involve themselves at one time or another. Such an area is Tenayuca. Here the lower class of people live quietly, hardly moved by the great metropolis of Mexico City, as significant as it may be to the future of some of their children. The heart of Mexico City is just six miles from Tenayuca.

The history of Tenayuca starts with the Toltecs, nomadic Chichimec Indians who moved into the Tenayuca area sometime around the eleventh century. Shortly after, the great war lord Xólotl established Tenayuca as his capital. His son, Nopaltzin, succeeded him and was responsible for the construction of the pyramid with the two parallel stairways. The next two dynastic rulers here, Tlohtzin and Quinatzin, adopted Toltec

93

customs, established Nahuatl as the official language, and enlarged their domain by conquests. Aztec ascendency in the Valley of Mexico eclipsed Tenayuca's strength and its economic importance. One of the last governors at Tenayuca was the baptized son of Moctezuma II, Rodrígo de Paz Moctezuma.

One of the best architectural examples of "superimpositions" in Mesoamerica is at Tenayuca. Here is a pyramid temple-structure that has eight superimpositions, a system of enlarging structures by covering the original building with rubble, and then constructing a great structure over it. This process would then be repeated at various cycles of the calendar, such as the beginning of the fifty-two year count. Sometimes new constructions would be undertaken because of the ascendance of a new ruler or for some other important event of the time. The structures that were "buried" because of the superimposition were often left intact, much to the delight of future archaeologists. The date of the innermost temple here has not been determined. The first two pyramids are in a local style. The third is in a transitional style, showing some Aztec influence. The remainder of the superimpositions are Aztec. The reconstructions at Tenayuca probably follow the cyclical fifty-two-year ceremonies that took place in 1299, 1351, 1403, 1455, and 1507. The height of the pyramid after the seventh superimposition is seventy feet. With its two temples on the top, it could have been twenty to thirty feet higher. The base of the structure covers approximately an acre of ground. The last superimposition (except for the grand staircase) was removed during reconstruction, and the visible pyramid today is the seventh superimposition.

Surrounding the great pyramid on three sides is a wall of unbroken serpents (138 in all) known as the Coatepantli, which must have produced a startling total effect when painted in brilliant colors. However, the workmanship is quite slap-dash in execution, reflecting the vigorous personality of the Toltecs at this time. The colors of the serpents had special significance that was related to the two temples on the pyramid. The serpents on the south and half of those on the east side were

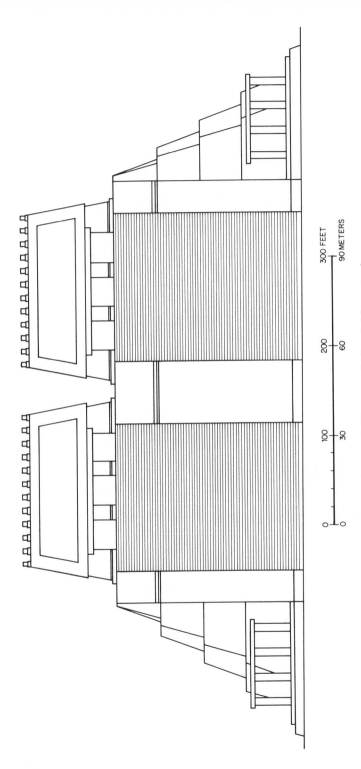

Tenayuca Pyramid, Elevation (After I. Marquina)

0   100   200   300 FEET

0   30   60   90 METERS

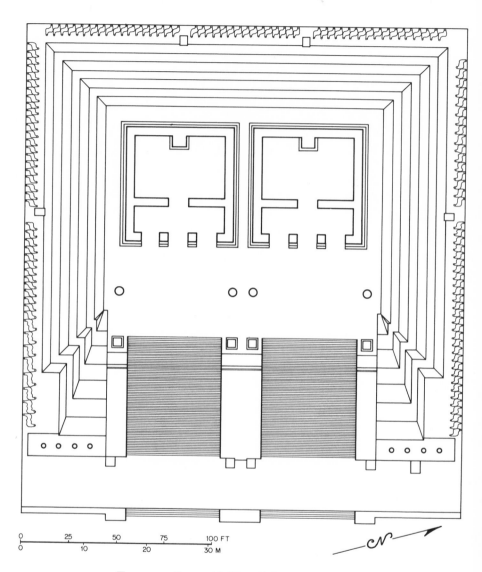

Tenayuca Pyramid, Plan (After I. Marquina)

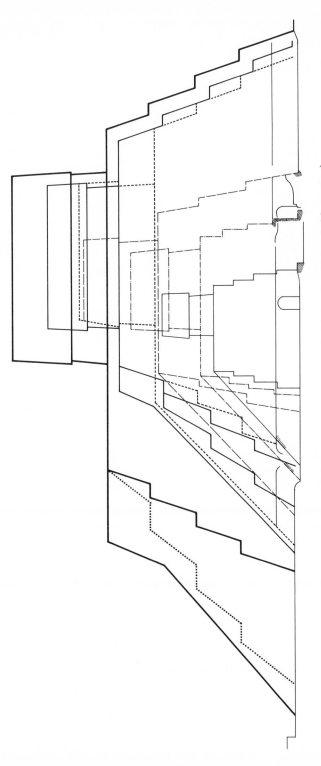

Tenayuca Pyramid, Cross Section Showing Superimpositions (After I. Marquina)

Model of the Tenayuca pyramid at the Museum of Anthropology in Mexico City. The temple on the left was dedicated to Tláloc, and the other to Huitzilopochtli. Only the base of the pyramid remains today. Postclassic.

Tenayuca pyramid showing the stairway to the last superimposition. Toltec. Postclassic.

The wall of serpents, Coatepantli, that encircles three sides of the Tenayuca pyramid. Postclassic.

painted green with black outlines for scales. Serpents on the north side and the other half of those on the east side were painted red on the lower part and black with white circles on the upper part. These were also the color symbols for day and night and north and south. One of the pyramids (on the left) was dedicated to Tláloc, the God of Rain, and the other was dedicated to the God of War, Huitzilopochtli. The latter temple was also known as "hummingbird on the left," a phrase taken from a legend. The exterior roof cornice of the Tláloc temple was decorated with vertical bands, while the Temple

99

The wall of serpents is raised on a platform that also supports the Tenayuca pyramid.

of the Sun was decorated with human skulls carved in stone and tenoned into the roof cornice. In some temples, such as that at Santa Cecilia, the skull was represented by a circular projection in which the features of the skull are not represented. The temples had roofs of wood, which can be best seen in the interior of the temple at Santa Cecilia.

This dramatic pyramid faces west and is aligned to the cardinal points with a seventeen-degree deviation. By looking directly west, the sun sets at this point on May 19 and July 26 — the time the sun passes through the zenith. It is quite possible that this particular pyramid was dedicated to the setting sun. The exterior walls of the temples, as well as the walls of the pyramid platform, were decorated with hundreds of heads of serpents which were tenoned into the walls. The

Two large curled serpents located on the north and east sides of the Tenayuca pyramid are believed to have faced the setting sun on the days of the solstices.

whole pyramid and the sculptures were then covered with a thin coating of lime and painted.

There are two large curled serpents adjacent to the north and east sides of the pyramid which are called Xiuhcóatl. Each of the serpents has a large voluted crest on its head with starlike projections on the edge of the crest. It is believed that the serpents faced the setting sun on the days of the solstices and were related to the renewal of fire. However, these sculptures were in such disrepair at the time of excavation that it was hard to determine the exact head direction.

The stairway to the last superimposition has several carved

Stairway to the sixth superimposition at Tenayuca, the one used today to climb to the top of the pyramid. The double stairway is separated by wide ramps.

stones, used on the step facings, that are not located in their original position. The designs are Aztec year signs, shields with spears, and other symbols familiar in Mixtec codices. It is believed that they belonged to an earlier structure and were reused. This great double stairway is in typical Aztec style, bordered by very low ramps. To the right of the stairway is a small altar called the Skull Altar. It is decorated with projecting skulls tenoned into the vertical wall. At one time the interior walls were decorated with a painted fresco of skulls and crossbones, but they have since disappeared.

The Aztec temples at Tenochtitlán, Tlatelolco, and Teopanzolco must have been modeled from the Tenayuca temple, since they are later in date and the architecture, technique, and subject matter are identical. At these sites are seen the use of the double stairway, the twin pyramids, and the double balustrade broken by vertical cubes. Ball courts were similar too. The Aztec temples are largely copies of these earlier Toltec structures.

The approach to the top of the pyramid is reached from the north side, where the original stair to the sixth superimposition has been reconstructed. The basalt stone used here has been dressed and mortared. This reddish-colored volcanic stone was at one time plastered and painted. The independent stairway in the very front of this pyramid is all that remains of the last superimposition, the rest of the last pyramid having long since disappeared.

To the east of the pyramid is a small museum that contains some of the artifacts found during excavation. Here one can see an artist's rendering of the various superimpositions of the pyramid. Also there are shields with spears carved in stone that were at one time tenoned into the building structure. Carved skulls from both Tenayuca and Santa Cecilia are scattered about the museum. There are also a few examples of local pottery.

Just a short drive of approximately two miles through narrow, winding streets leads to Santa Cecilia. Little is known of the site, but at one time it must have been the center of another Aztec conclave. Now the pyramid of Santa Cecilia is hemmed in by the high walls of villagers' compounds that have encroached very close to the walls of the pyramid.

In the late afternoon the setting sun lightens the façade of Santa Cecilia in a glow of golden sunshine. This is really the time to see this small Aztec shrine. There is no other complete Aztec temple in existence. The most that the visitor is seeing at Tenayuca, Teopanzolco, and Zempoala are the platforms to the important buildings they once supported, although at Teopanzolco are the partial remains of the side walls of the two temples. Many years ago when the traveler approached Santa Cecilia, the most he could expect to see was a great earthen hill sparsely covered with grass. When archaeologists began uncovering the great mound, they soon realized that the outer shell that was the last superimposition was in

Santa Cecilia pyramid. The temple on the top is the only Aztec temple in existence. Postclassic period.

a very poor state of repair. The stones of the pyramid had been removed at some earlier time for village construction. When the workers dug deeper into the mound, they were greatly surprised to find another inner superimposition, a structure that had been built earlier, but possibly no earlier than the fifty-two-year cycle. This structure was a double-staired pyramid that was at one time surmounted by two temples, one of which had also been dismantled by the villagers for their own purposes. Many of the churches and other public buildings at Tenayuca and Santa Cecilia are constructed of stones salvaged from earlier structures built by the Aztecs. Nevertheless, the remaining sanctuary that was dedicated to Huitzilopochtli was completely intact. The Santa Cecilia pyramid is not a great one, and consequently the remaining sanctuary is not very large; however, the detail is interesting.

104

Another view of the pyramid at Santa Cecilia. At one time this struc-
ture had a twin pyramid and temple, but it was dismantled in colonial
times. Postclassic.

Just before reaching the pyramid is a long platform that at one time was the approach to the last superimposition. Going around this platform, the traveler can mount the stairway to the earlier temple. Looking upward, one can see two large urn-shaped pedestals constructed of small stones cemented together, placed on either side of the top platform. These may have held bowls for burning incense or a constant flame, creating a mystic quality to the temple entrance. The stairs are extremely steep, as most of the Aztec stairways seem to be, but they are not the high stairways one encounters at Teotihuacán or Cholula. The temple on top is small but complete. Archaeologists have reconstructed the interior of the roof so that the visitor can see the details of the poles and beams, and their placement before plastering. The temple has only one room with a stone bench against the back wall. The exterior roof is studded with curvilinear tenoned stones that are symbolic of the skulls sometimes fashioned for the Huitzilopochtli temple. The view from the temple doorway is one of tranquility as the setting sun sprinkles its rays of light through fragile hanging pepper-tree vines. In the distance can be heard the muted rustic sounds of villagers preparing for the evening activities.

Tlatelolco

In the heart of Mexico City excavations for a large housing project brought to light the ruins of Tlatelolco. This area is now called Plaza of the Three Cultures, referring to the present-day apartment structures, the old Spanish church, and the ancient ruins of Tlatelolco. These ruins are Aztec, and the structures are very similar to other Aztec centers such as Tenayuca, Tenochtitlán, and Teopanzolco. The whole style of Aztec architecture is derived from the Toltecs, and could very easily be called Toltecoid.

When the Aztecs entered the western region of Lake Texcoco in the fourteenth century, one group settled on the south

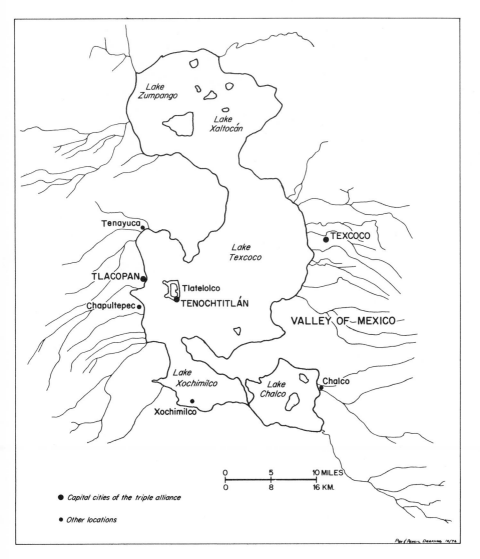

Valley of Mexico During Aztec Rule

The Aztec ruins, the colonial Spanish church, and the present-day apartment structures make up the Plaza of Three Cultures where the ancient Aztec city of Tlatelolco was located.

island and another on the north island, the first eventually becoming the occupants of Tenochtitlán and the latter of Tlatelolco. These two areas eventually were joined when this swamp region was filled in for *chinampas;* however, they remained politically independent from Tenochtitlán until late in the fifteenth century when Tlatelolco was conquered, the people humiliated, and the city partially destroyed because of the avaricious power politics of the ruling families at Tenochtitlán.

Tlatelolco is described by the Spaniards as an extremely important city for trade and marketing with as many as 20,000 to 25,000 persons gathered daily. This ancient city had a great number of craft guilds, and much of the population was employed as craft specialists. Most food for the city had to be

The circular adoratorio *at Tlatelolco is located in front of a double platform that was the base for a temple when the Aztec empire was at its height. Postclassic.*

imported. The commercial center of Tlatelolco was enhanced by the great canoe fleet of the Tlatelolcoans. It not only speeded trade items to and from the market, but it could be used for war as well.

Today the ruins of Tlatelolco look more like a park with walks and stairs on which the visitor may stroll as he views the ancient ruins. These foundations have been restored, and the area holds some interest. Here are dozens of platforms, made of volcanic stone and cement, that unavoidably have been sinking farther into the ground since the land at one time was a swamp. These platforms indicate the general shape of the buildings of the time. We can see the twin pyramid complex was in use, very similar to that at Tenayuca, only smaller. There are several round temple platforms that may have been temples devoted to the Wind God, Ehécatl, or Coat-

109

Part of the Plaza of Tlatelolco showing the platforms for Aztec temples and other structures. Postclassic.

licue, the Earth Goddess. Some of the round platforms may also have been used for religious or secular ceremonies. The long rectangular platforms to one side of the plaza may have been part of the commercial center or a part of the market area. On one small altar was found the remains of a mural of skulls and crossbones similar to the mural that existed at one time inside the altar of skulls at Tenayuca. This small scrap of painting is our only indication that Aztec buildings may have had murals.

On one of the platforms near the Main Temple at Tlatelolco are carved, in separate panels, a series of thirty-nine calendric

This Aztec circular pyramid structure was discovered when excavations began for the subway in Mexico City. Postclassic.

dates or dates that signify calendric deities. These carvings act as a cornice frieze on three sides of a structure now designated as the Templo Calendárico.

Since we know that Tlatelolco was a magnificent city, it does not seem possible that hardly a vestige of these ancient ruins is left to give us some idea of its magnitude. This is also true of Tenochtitlán. To see how little remains of this truly great city bewilders and shocks any member of the human race.

One block from the cathedral in Mexico City was discovered a portion of the main ceremonial center of Tenochtitlán buried far below the level of the street. It was uncovered during the digging for the foundation of a building. The area has been set aside as a small outdoor museum. This portion of the ruins of Tenochtitlán is believed to be part of the Templo Mayor.

111

Sections of the walls, platforms, and the stairway can be seen. Also, there is a very large brazier *in situ* that is decorated with a bow. Large sculptures were also found in this location, but they have since been removed to the Museum of Anthropology.

In excavating for the new subway, a short distance from the cathedral an ancient circular platform was discovered. This platform was also restored and can now be seen in one of Mexico City's modern subway stations. Tenochtitlán was completely destroyed by the Spaniards and the stones were used to build the new city of Mexico. The rest of Tenochtitlán lies buried far below the present city, lost for all time.

III Valley of Toluca

Malinalco

Matlalac is on the crest of the *Montes de Mixtongo*. This very high point of the mountain pass, wild with the wind and the craggy outcroppings, offers a view of the remote town of Malinalco far below, hemmed in a tropical valley. From here the narrow, rough, dirt road winds down along the edge of the cliffs until it reaches the verdant valley floor. The altitude is a little over six thousand feet, creating a warm but pleasant climate. The village has not changed from colonial times as few "outsiders" get to see this part of Mexico even though it is only a short distance from Toluca, famous for its Friday market.

From the village of Malinalco the impressive Aztec ruins, referred to locally as the *Cerro de los Idolos*, can be seen high on the escarpment of the mountains. The walk to the site takes approximately half an hour up a narrow, steep, winding path. As one approaches the top, the view is spectacular. The Aztecs who built this ceremonial site had a commanding view of any persons or armies entering this rich, prosperous valley.

It was during the rule of the Aztec emperor Axayacatl that Malinalco was conquered—less than one hundred years before the Spaniards arrived. The construction of the ceremonial center high on this mountain ledge continued over a long period of years (1476–1520), and it was still incomplete when the Spaniards arrived. Cortés sent a detachment of troops to seize the fortifications and the valley, burning what could be destroyed by fire. Fortunately, the foundations of the structures were cut out of living rock and not easily despoiled. The beauty of the site lies in the unique chambers and remarkable stone carvings carefully cut by the stonecutters so that even today they are still a part of the living rock. Malinalco typifies Aztec

113

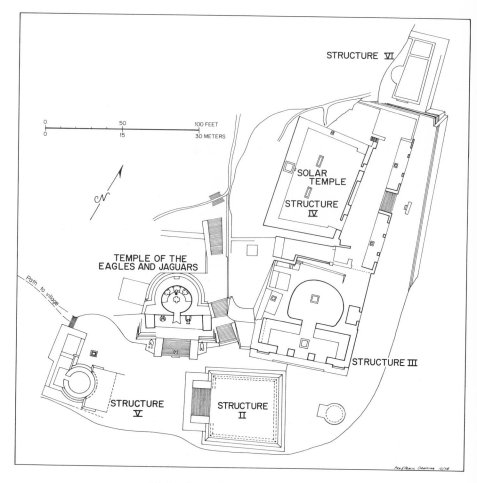

Malinalco (After J. García Payón)

expression in sculpture and architecture. Even though sculptures are symbolic, they are carved in a realistic style, refined,
and suggest a precise simplicity that gives great strength and
vigor. The mastery over stone is one of the great accomplishments of the Aztec craftsmen. Simple forms in sculpture were
successfully combined with extensive decorative surface

114

Structure 1, Temple of the Eagles and Jaguar, Malinalco. This important building is carved out of living stone and has a reconstructed roof of thatch. Postclassic.

carving. The finished sculpture was further enhanced by the refined surface treatment, whether it was a mat or a high-polished finish.

The most important structure at Malinalco is Structure I, the Temple of the Eagles and Jaguar. The Aztecs also referred to it as the Temple of the Sun, Cuacuahtinchan. The Instituto Nacional de Antropologia e Historia undertook restoration at Malinalco in 1936, and one of the first structures to receive attention was the Temple of the Eagles and Jaguar. A thatch-and-wood roof was constructed that might have been typical of the type used by the Aztecs prior to the Spanish Conquest. This helped to protect the sculptures within the temple. The reddish-brown rock from which the temple is carved is a soft volcanic tuft easily affected by erosion.

Flanked by wide ramps, a short flight of steps leads to the

115

Jaguar carved out of the living stone on the interior of Structure 1 at Malinalco. Postclassic.

temple's unique doorway. Pedestals on platforms on either side of the stairway hold the remains of two sculptured jaguars. On the center of the stairs are the remains of an anthropomorphic figure, badly defaced, that may have been a standard bearer. On either side of the top platform are two additional sculptures. On the left is a jaguar seated on a drum, and on the right are the remains of an eagle knight resting on a large serpent head.

The great doorway, carved in a vigorous, cursive style, represents what seems to be a great open mouth of a fantastic serpent with huge eyes and fangs. The doorway, symbolically, might also suggest the earth deity with its mouth open, seemingly ready to receive the knightly persons who may enter. The approach to the doorway is on the flattened forked tongue of the serpent that stretches through the doorway and acts as a carpet for any approaching guests. Within the arch is a most

116

Eagle sculpture in the Temple of the Eagles and Jaguar, Malinalco. Postclassic.

unusual circular chamber with a bench encircling the room, all carved out of the living rock. This extraordinary room is then enhanced with four major sculptures representing a jaguar and three eagles beautifully carved in the living stone. They are only the sculptured skins of the animals stretched out along the circular bench and the floor of the room. Since they are carved very realistically, the dim light in the room gives them a quality of being alive. Nowhere has a chamber ever been carved like this. Originally, all the sculptures, both inside and outside this sacred chamber, were given a fine coating of lime and then painted. The Temple of the Eagles and Jaguar was an extremely important and sacred place for the military rank. It was in this chamber that initiation and dedicatory ceremonies took place in which young noblemen pledged their lives to their gods, their leaders, and their empire. The ceremony of piercing the nose in order to insert the fang of a jaguar

Structure III, Malinalco. The remains of a two-chambered building carved out of living stone. In Mesoamerica the Aztec site of Malinalco was the only ceremonial center carved out of living rock.

or the claw of the eagle took place in this sacred room.

The Temple of the Eagles and Jaguar was only one of the many structures that made up the complex to house and serve the purposes of this military organization. Just to the south of this structure are the remains of the foundation of a circular structure that may have been the temple dedicated to Ehécatl, or the temple of Quetzalcoatl. Probably the second most important building here is Structure III, which is adjacent to the main temple. This two-room structure is also carved into the mountain, with rooms formed of the living stone. The large rectangular entrance room was at one time painted with beautiful murals of the stellar deities walking on a wide band of feathers and jaguar skins, but little indication of these remain today. Surrounding the room are benches along the east, west, and north walls. The second room to the north is circular, and both rooms have small altars placed in the center area of the floor. Structure III is said to be the area where ceremonies for cremation and deification of the dead knights took place.

By climbing up the monolithic stairways to the backs of these chambers, one can appreciate the drainage system for this ceremonial center. During the rainy season, water rushes down the numerous ravines high above the site. To avoid this yearly flooding, the Aztecs cut extremely deep drainage channels into the stone to direct the water around the various structures. Part of this little engineering feat can be observed by walking along the cliffs to the north of the ceremonial area.

To the north of Structure III is the Solar Temple, Structure IV, partially hewn out of solid rock and facing the east. Again the chamber's walls have benches that may have been for seating, or they could have served many other purposes. Multipurpose rooms are not unusual in Mesoamerica. Areas could quickly be converted from an eating or sleeping space to storage areas or places for council meetings. There are two altars on either side of the room not too different from those in Structure III. Archaeologists have established that the roof was split in two sections resting on beams at different levels, permitting the sun's rays to illuminate the back of the chamber and leaving the rest of the structure in darkness. Directing the light in this way must have served some ceremonial purpose for the order of knights who used the room. Since this military organization was also known as the Knights of the Sun, the significance of the sun in their military organization as a religious deity and as an important economic factor in agriculture becomes apparent. It is believed that this temple was used for the great feast of the sun—a celebrated day (Nahui Olin) in the Aztec calendar when an important person was sacrificed.

Just to the north of the Solar Temple is Structure VI, one of several structures that were never finished. This ceremonial center was still being built when the assault came from the Spaniards. Also left unfinished were parts of retaining walls, built ingeniously from the rock and rubble carved out of the

119

Stairways carved into the mountain served the Aztecs for access to the Malinalco ceremonial center and fort. Grooves on the stairs served to channel the water from the mountainside to the rocky cliffs.

Structure IV at Malinalco is the Solar Temple used by the Aztecs in the fifteenth century.

mountain. Many sections of the retaining walls are the solid core of the mountain. Where height was needed, the stone and rubble were added until the desired level was reached for the platforms and plazas. Malinalco clings from the sides of these cliffs like an eagle's nest hanging over the ruptured edge of steep precipices higher in the mountains.

Calixtlahuaca

The Matlazinca people living in the Valley of Toluca have been fortunate in having one of the richest, most fertile valleys for corn growing in the highlands. In pre-Columbian times they were the most unfortunate of people in being situated between

121

two warring factions, the Aztecs to the northeast and the Tarascans to the west, both desirous of control over this abundant food bowl. Over the turbulent centuries, the Matlazincas maintained their independence as far as they possibly could, but at no time was it to last very long.

Little is known of the early peoples in the Valley of Toluca in Preclassic time. There is some indication of Teotihuacán influence in Classic times. The early Postclassic stage (A.D. 900–1200) may have been either dominated by the Toltecs from Tula or have come under their influence. The Matlazincas used the Toltec calendar and place names, and their architecture certainly suggests Toltec prototypes.

Calixtlahuaca, "Place Where There are Houses on the Prairie," has been occupied by Matlazinca-speaking peoples at least as far back as the Early Postclassic period. The archaeological zone is located on the left bank of the Tejalpa River between the town of Tecaxic and Calixtlahuaca. In ancient times the people lived among the cultivated fields in the plains. During raids and times of war, the populace would flee to the nearby terraced hill fortifications. Granaries behind the forts supplied ample food until these conflicts were over.

Excavations were first started at Calixtlahuaca in 1930 and continued until 1938. The hill area where Structure 3 (Temple of Quetzalcoatl) is located was heavily terraced and fortified. After the Aztec occupation, the terraces were enlarged, joined, and new structures added for ceremonial use. Also, the area was more heavily fortified. The nearby mountains were a prime source for the porous volcanic stone (tezontle) used for construction here.

Before the Aztecs entered their valley, the Matlazincas knew they could not hold out against both the warring Tarascans and the greedy Aztecs hungry for more land. Unfortunately, the three great chiefs of the Toluca Valley were in disagreement, not knowing whether to try to remain independent or to join one of the two warring factions. It was the Aztec emperor, Axacacatl, who did not hesitate to attack the Matlazincas in one of the most brutal battles of Aztec history in which over eleven thousand prisoners were taken for sacrifice to Tenochtitlán. After confiscation of much of the land, the Emperor had hundreds of Aztec families moved to the Toluca Valley for settlement. Calixtlahuaca was the center for this movement, and a new military garrison was established there by the Aztecs. The following year the adjoining valley, Malinalco, fell to the conquering Aztecs. Following these conquests were many rebellions. One of these is recorded in a great stone monument, the Tizoc Stone. It was the short-lived Aztec emperor Tizoc who entered the Toluca Valley, squashing rebellions, demanding higher tributes, and taking prisoners for sacrifice who had the Tizoc Stone carved in his honor. The stone can now be seen in the Museum of Anthropology in Mexico City. The last rebellion in the Toluca Valley was in 1510 when Moctezuma II entered the valley and saw to the destruction of the Matlazincas. Shortly afterward, the entry of the Spaniards freed them from this yoke, only to be again enslaved by another type of subservient harness, colonialism.

Although the archaeological area of Calixtlahuaca is very extensive, reaching far into the Toluca Valley, the major constructions are confined to the hill terraces and adjacent plain. These hill terraces were reinforced by stone retaining walls. Ramps and stairways were constructed so that the various terraces could be joined, creating access passages from one terrace to another. García Payón carried out extensive excavations here, noting a characteristic Matlazinca pottery using geometric designs in polychrome. Commonly found was an open bowl with tripod legs. This pottery has also been found at Malinalco, indicating trade with the next valley. This particular pottery is of the Early Postclassic period.

The larger terraces higher on the hillside were selected by the Aztecs for construction of their major temples. However, the confinement of the narrow terraces meant that there was no possibility of having the large plazas and courtyards so familiar in other areas. Here, the most important temple is the Temple of Quetzalcoatl. The archaeological zone has seventeen major mounds, many of them enclosed by farmlands. Some

Temple of the Wind, Calixtlahuaca. There are four superimpositions within the temple structure. Postclassic period.

have been excavated either partially or completely. There are vestiges of old retaining walls at Calixtlahuaca that date from Preclassic time. Other walls and platforms indicate occupation during the Classic period. Major constructions here are of Toltec style dating from the Postclassic period (A.D. 900–1500). However, it was the Aztecs who built most of the structures during their last century of occupation.

Rising high against the hill of green terraced fields is the Temple of Quetzalcoatl (Structure 3) dedicated to the Wind God, Ehécatl. The building has four superimpositions, all round, constructed of different materials. The earliest superimposition is a small-roomed structure with a ramped stairway which can be seen by entering a tunnel on the north side of the pyramid. This early structure is believed to be of Teotihuacán style and may have been constructed sometime between the fifth and seventh centuries, setting the style for round buildings so popular during the Toltec-Aztec occupation of the Valley of Mexico. The second superimposition of this pyramid is in the Toltec style and has similarities to the structure El Corral at Tula. The third superimposition, built of dressed andesite, is

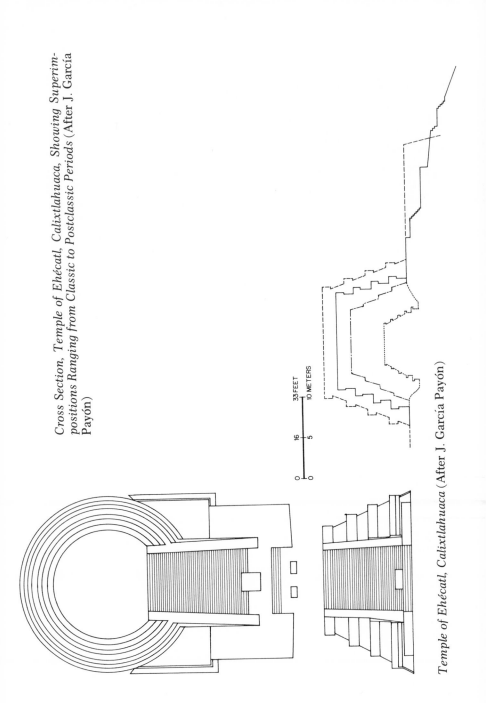

Cross Section, Temple of Ehécatl, Calixtlahuaca, Showing Superim-positions Ranging from Classic to Postclassic Periods (After J. García Payón)

Temple of Ehécatl, Calixtlahuaca (After J. García Payón)

larger and there is some indication that it was destroyed by the earthquake of 1475. The last superimposition is also round, having four platforms with deep cornices. The stairway, facing east, is edged with a wide ramp, and the ascent to the top is forty feet. In the center of the platform a rectangular altar was installed. This last superimposition is Aztec. It is of interest to note that Quetzalcoatl as God of the Wind was a deity of such importance that he was respected as a benevolent deity throughout three great periods of Mesoamerican history extending over one thousand years.

A rare find for archaeologists was the large statue of Ehécatl buried in the south side of the platform. This impressive stone sculpture has all the characteristics of the vigor, vitality, and simplicity Aztec sculptors could envision, making their sculpture their greatest craft. The sculpture, carved in andesite, is a representation of a man wearing a loin cloth, sandals, and a mask in the form of a bird's beak, a portrayal that typified the god Ehécatl. The sculpture is now in the collection of the State Archaeological Museum in Toluca.

One of the most interesting complexes at Calixtlahuaca is that unit comprised of the Temple of Tláloc (Structure 4), Structure 7, and the Altar of Skulls, all of which are built of red and black pumice stone. The temple of Tláloc had four platforms, but only two of them exist today. The temple is approached by a stairway with ramps similar to the stairway of the Temple of Quetzalcoatl. Structure 7 is a low platform having a stairway spanning nearly the entire front of the platform. The kind of structure that once rested on the platform is unknown, although it could have been a palace-type structure for one of the Aztec overlords.

The last of the Aztec structures in this complex is a small monument called the Altar of the Skulls. The base of the Altar

Facing page: *God of the Wind. Ehécatl, in the Museum of Anthropology in Mexico City. This sculpture is similar to the one found in the interior of the Temple of the Wind, Calixtlahuaca. Postclassic.*

Part of the ruins of Calixtlahuaca once occupied by the powerful Matlazinca Indians. Postclassic.

is cruciform in shape with one arm of the cruciform semicircular. The entire structure has rows of stone skulls and curved knobs of stone which are tenoned into the cruciform vertical walls. This platform is approximately six feet in height. The two chambers on the inside held the remains of ashes, possibly indicating that the structure was dedicated to the death of the sun, a ceremony that was performed at the end of the fifty-two-year cycle.

A complex of structures (known as Structure 17) which surrounds an open court is referred to as the "*calmecac,*" an Aztec educational institution. The structures surrounding the court are many and varied, with altars, temples, storage rooms, hallways, and other living spaces that may have been multiple in purpose. Excavation revealed that the structure was one of the many buildings that was burned when Moctezuma II ordered the destruction of villages that were causing rebellions in this valley.

Many other existing platforms are all that are now left of the archaeological zone of Calixtlahuaca. Beautiful Aztec sculptures and other artifacts have been found in the area, some of them now housed in the State Archaeological Museum in Toluca.

IV Valley of Morelos

Xochicalco

The drive along the highway from Mexico City to Cuernavaca reveals some of Mexico's finest mountain and valley landscapes. Great pine forests break the cloud patterns of the misty wind-swept sky. Many miles beyond the horizon the highway drops to a lower elevation and then stretches into the warm, subtropical valley of Cuernavaca. This small valley in the state of Morelos has always been a haven for man. There is abundant water from the nearby mountains, a rich fertile valley for agriculture, and sufficient wildlife in the forests and streams to supply meat for families over the many centuries. Indians must have fought desperately to keep their lands from the migrating tribal peoples passing through the valley.

From Cuernavaca the distance to Xochicalco is approximately twenty-eight miles. After passing lush farm growth, the road gradually ascends to rugged hillside terrain, winding between craggy rock outcroppings until the site of Xochicalco is reached. The archaeological ruins spread over a large group of hilltops artificially shaped into a series of stone terraces and platforms. The hilltop site not only was a ceremonial center, but also may have served as a political capital and a residential area for some of the elite. The major area, the Acropolis, is covered with ceremonial structures and residences that would indicate a dense population. The hill to the northeast, known as Cerro de Bodego, has a walled platform and may have been a more specialized ceremonial center. There is some indication that it could have served as a fort. The populace must have lived in hamlets throughout the valley where they could more easily concern themselves with agriculture, trade, and home

industries. William T. Sanders estimates the population to
have been between ten and twenty thousand persons.

The archaeological site of Xochicalco extends over hillsides covering more than six hundred acres. Stone walls and
moats curving around broad terraces suggest the importance
of this site as a military post. Although the more important
structures are on the crests of the hills, many mounds can be
seen extending far below this area. Only a very small section
of this massive hill complex has been excavated. Occupied
from Late Classic to Postclassic times, the site came under the
influence of the major Classic cultures that preceded it—the
Maya, Teotihuacán, Classic Veracruz, and Monte Albán.
Recent archaeological excavations give some idea of the extent
of cultural contact.

Little is known about who the actual inhabitants of Xochicalco were. From earliest time this valley lay in the migration
route of peoples moving from the Pacific coastal area to the
Mexican highlands. It is quite possible that some of these
people were related to the Chichimec tribal groups or Nahuatl
speaking peoples who later established themselves as the Toltecs. Another area from which these people might have originated is the Mixtec-Puebla confluence in the area of Cholula.
Here, in Late Classic time, the Mixtecs were expanding into
the southern Zapotec area, and might well have moved into
other valley areas such as Xochicalco. Artifacts found at Xochicalco certainly indicate trade with Cholula. Also, both Zapotec
and Mixtec glyphs were utilized on monuments. When Teotihuacán collapsed in the seventh century, migrant groups,
believed to have been Toltecs, moved into that fertile valley.
The influence of Teotihuacán on the Toltec culture as well as
that at Xochicalco is noted in their architecture and minor
crafts. Xochicalco is comparable in size and contemporary with
Tula, the Toltec capital, if we allow for an earlier developmental
period. J. R. Acosta, a Mexican archaeologist, has suggested
such an antique phase at Tula that began as early as A.D. 700.
This would also be approximately the beginning of construc-

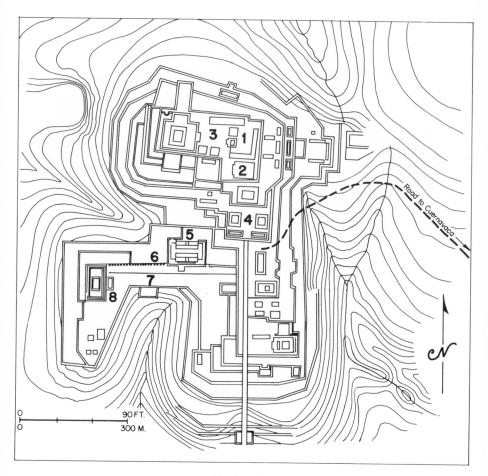

Xochicalco

tion at Xochicalco. Both cultural areas were in existence until close to the end of the twelfth century.

The most important pyramid at Xochicalco is the Pyramid of the Plumed Serpent. It is located on a large plaza at the very summit of the terraced platforms. From this vantage point, it is readily seen that the ceremonial center was oriented to the

Pyramid of the Plumed Serpent, Xochicalco. The talud of this unusual structure is decorated in relief carvings. Postclassic.

cardinal points, a type of orientation that is not always practical on terraced hillsides. Farther south in the Maya area the hilltop sites were more apt to follow patterns of the natural terrain than the cardinal directions. This was especially true at Yaxchilán and Pedras Negras.

A short distance from the Pyramid of the Plumed Serpent, a path going north leads down a steep hillside to a series of natural caves. Over the centuries these caves were occupied from time to time. A funnel to a small hole in the roof of one cave permits the sun to penetrate during the equinoxes. We can only assume that the Indians used these caves as astronomical observation posts in their remote past.

The Pyramid of the Plumed Serpent was one of the first structures to be restored at Xochicalco in 1910 under the direction of Leopoldo Batres. Restoration continued in 1961. The building is not complete, as the walls of the temple on top of the platform are in partial repair. The architectural style of this platform is consistent with other structures at Xochicalco. The Pyramid of the Plumed Serpent is the most handsomely carved structure at Xochicalco. This pyramid and some of the other major structures here could date back as early as the

Corner of the talud *on the Pyramid of the Plumed Serpent, Xochicalco.*

ninth century. The *talud* (inclined base) becomes the larger architectural wall of the pyramid. Here sculptors lavishly portrayed the rulers, priests, knights, and deities in a baroque, curvilinear-styled bas-relief. Encircling the pyramid are eight undulating feathered serpents covering the entire *talud*. Seashells are encrusted on their backs as well as their bodies. Approximately six centuries earlier a similar serpent was carved on the walls of the Pyramid of Quetzalcoatl at Teotihuacán. At Xochicalco the style of the stone carving reflects the baroque southern style of the Late Classic Mayas. It is a sophisticated art form with clear, crisp lines demonstrating a high technical excellence.

Between the undulations of the body of the serpent are seated dignitaries dressed in loincloths and with elaborate headdresses of quetzal feathers, necklaces, bracelets, anklets,

134

A seated figure between the undulations of the plumed serpent on the Pyramid of the Plumed Serpent, Xochicalco. Postclassic.

and earrings that may have represented jade. The position of the seated dignitary and the style of carving are nearly identical to that on Alter Q at Copán. Other sculptural decorative forms located between the body of the serpent are glyphic in design. The fire glyph is especially evident.

Above this dramatic *talud* is a cornice shaped into a *tablero*, and decorated in a bas-relief of sculptured seated figures and associated glyphs. The coyote also features prominently in these reliefs. Some archaeologists believe the figures to be priests, and they might well be; however, they are not too unlike the seated dignitaries on the *talud* just below. A terminal molding to this cornice is decorated in a stylized shell motif, and projects well beyond the *tablero*. Exaggerated flaring cornices of this type are well known at the site of El Tajín in

135

Below the trail of the serpent is the fire glyph with the numeral 9. Pyramid of the Plumed Serpent, Xochicalco.

Veracruz and their builders may have influenced the architects at Xochicalco.

On the top platform of the Pyramid is a partial reconstruction of the main temple walls. Originally the building had a flat roof constructed of wooden beams which were then plastered. Sculpture here depicts warriors holding square shields and arrows and wearing elaborate headdresses. Interspersed with these warriors are coyotes, eagles, and other indications of an allegiance to knightly orders so popular among the Toltecs. Reconstruction is "sketchy" here, for some of the carved stones are obviously not placed in their original position.

There has been considerable speculation on the nature of

the glyphs on the west end of the Pyramid. On the left side of the stairway, a complicated composite glyph arrangement shows a hand reaching from behind a "house" glyph grasping a rope that is tied to a "monkey" glyph. The other hand rests on a numeral "one" glyph. According to Eduardo Noguera this represents some adjustment to the calendar. However, with such brief glyphic data as this, it would seem that some other abstract idea could well be represented. Glyphs in both the Zapotec or Maya and Nahuatl or Mixtec systems of writing are incorporated in this glyphic block.

The short stairway has balustrades that are decorated with a serpent motif in which the ventral scales of the serpent are indicated. This particular design is unique to this extraordinary temple.

Faced with veneered slabs of andesite stone, the Pyramid of the Plumed Serpent was originally given a thin coat of lime plaster and then painted. Traces of green, red, white, blue, and black have been noted. This was covered over at a later time with a solid coat of red paint. Today the traveler sees only the darkened basalt stone, for the paint has long since disappeared. This is the only structure excavated so far at Xochicalco which has been completely sculptured in bas-relief. Aesthetically the bas-relief on the Pyramid of the Plumed Serpent is one of America's important sculptural achievements.

Adjacent to the Pyramid of the Plumed Serpent is another larger platformed structure referred to as Structure A, but also called the Temple of the Stelae because of stelae found here. On its right corner is an oratory-type structure not unlike those used at Tulúm by the Mayas. A short flight of steps to Structure A leads to a multiple-room building. Only the foundation of this building is here today, but the floor plan is easily seen. In the center of the structure is an open, sunken patio. Porticoed chambers are located around the patio. This plan is not unlike the Palace of Quetzalpapalotl at Teotihuacán. At the east end of the building is a small sanctuary. During excavation of the floor, César A. Saenz discovered three beautifully preserved stelae as well as many artifacts buried in a sealed chamber.

137

Temple of the Stelae, Structure A, where three monuments were found buried under the temple, Xochicalco. Postclassic.

Among them were small figurines in the Teotihuacán style, shell and turquoise, beads of jade, human bones, spear points of obsidian, and part of an onyx mask. The chamber may have been constructed purposely to bury these treasures from other conquering peoples sometime during the Late Classic or early Postclassic period.

The three stelae are approximately five feet high and carved on all four sides. The two deities represented on them are Quetzalcoatl and Tláloc. A series of calendric glyphs in Zapotec and Mixtec style are carved on the vertical sides of the monuments. These stelae have been removed from the site and are now located in the Museum of Anthropology in Mexico City. Later additions were made to Structure A on the south and west sides such as small rooms, platforms, and altars.

138

These structural changes probably reflect the need for increased facilities as this stratified society struggled to serve the multiplying population.

South of Structure A is another large plaza located on a terraced area approximately fifty feet lower in elevation. Two small temple structures at either end of the plaza have been partially restored. A great staircase on the north side of this plaza flanks a very large pyramid that has not been excavated. From the top of this pyramid is a splendid view of the Morelos Valley and the beautiful round lake, El Rodeo, that lies on the horizon. Toward the east the many distant hilltops covered with unexcavated mounds can be spotted.

In the center of the plaza is a raised platform that is the base for a large, rectangular stela a little over six feet high and carved with two large blocks of glyphs. The style has no similarities to the three stelae found in Structure A. Although there is no way of dating this stone monument, it must have been erected considerably earlier and surely must have had great significance to the hierarchy of the time to deserve this honored position. The monument was discovered inside the mound in the center of the plaza during excavation. Its original position is not known. Two plain stone yokes used in connection with ceremonies related to the ball game were also discovered in this mound. These yokes are another indication of the influence of the Veracruz Classic civilization. Careful inspection of the platform shows that it was enlarged at least once.

This plaza as well as the many others here were all plastered and painted. The buildings and sculpture were also painted.

On a terraced platform to the southwest, at a much lower elevation than this plaza, is one of the beautifully preserved ball courts at Xochicalco which has now been restored. The court is traditionally in the shape of a capital "I," and is over two hundred feet long. A narrow stairway on the east end of the court leads to the playing field. The side benches (slanted bases) used in playing the game are at a low angle compared to

Rectangular stela with two large glyph panels located in the plaza of the ceremonial center at Xochicalco.

Pyramid of the Niches, El Tajín. The back view of the pyramid shows the interesting series of niches that decorate the platforms. Classic Veracruz period.

The partially reconstructed Southern Ball Court at El Tajín. The vertical walls are decorated in sculptured low reliefs of ceremonies connected with the ball game. Classic period.

The ball court, Xochicalco. In the shape of a capital "I," the ball court has vertical side walls where rings are placed for scoring in the game. Postclassic period.

Thin orange jar with a fresco painting of the head of Tláloc, Teotihuacán. Classic period. Collection of The American Museum of Natural History, New York. Courtesy of the Museum.

Pathway of the Dead, Teotihuacán. Foreground platforms encircle the Plaza of the Moon. Pyramid of the Sun in the distance. Protoclassic and Classic periods.

Pyramid of the Sun, Teotihuacán. In the foreground recent excavations reveal administrative and palace-type structures. Protoclassic period.

Portion of the wall fresco being constructed in the Patio Blanco, Teotihuacán. The outline drawing has been reconstructed first. The original painted plaster will be adhered to the surface in the dark circles areas in the next step of reconstruction. Mural depicts a deity or knight dressed in an eagle costume.

he Great Vestibule and Pyramid of Quetzalcoatl at Tula. Toltec Postclassic period.

*Portion of a restored wall in the
Patio Blanco, Teotihuacán.
Tláloc, God of Water, is shown
wearing an elaborate bird
headdress, and he carries a
staff in his right hand. Early
Classic period.*

Olmec ceremonial adze of blue-gray jade, known as the Kunz adze, reported to have been found in the Oaxaca area. Middle Preclassic period. Collection of The American Museum of Natural History, New York. Courtesy of the Museum.

Mosaic jade carving of the bat deity found in the Main Plaza, Monte Albán. Late Preclassic Period. Collection of the Museo Nacional de Antropologia e Historia, Mexico City.

Mixtec disc of gold and precious stones discovered in Tomb 2, Zaachila. Postclassic period.

Detail of the wall painting in Tomb 105, Monte Albán, as reproduced in the Museo Nacional de Antropologia e Historia, Mexico City. The two persons may represent deities. Glyphs are interspersed between the design elements. Classic period.

Mural painting in fresco technique at Tomb 105, Monte Albán as reproduced in the Museo Nacional de Antropologia e Historia, Mexico City. A procession of gods and goddesses in elaborate ceremonial dress decorates the entrance. Classic period.

Entrance to Tomb 105 at Monte Albán. Frescos in the cruciform-shaped tomb are the finest at Monte Albán. Classic period.

Santa Cecilia is located near Tenayuca, and this pyramid has the only Aztec temple still extant. Postclassic period.

System 4, Monte Albán. An enclosed courtyard projects to the front of the main platform of System 4. A foundation of the original temple can be seen on the top of the platform. Classic period.

Danzante *stone relief at Monte Albán. Middle Preclassic period.*

The hillside site of Yagul located in the fertile valley area south of Mitla. The Mixtecs who settled this city are believed to have come from Lambityeco.

The great Pyramid of Cholula is a hillside of green vegetation. A colonial church is on top of the pyramid. In the foreground is part of the great plaza area.

The colonial church at Mitla, constructed in the courtyard of a Mixtec palace. Ancient stones from the palace were used to build the church. Postclassic period.

Pyramid of the Plumed Serpent, Xochicalco. Postclassic period.

Detail of the beautiful relief carved on the Pyramid of the Plumed Serpent, Xochicalco. Postclassic period.

Detail of the relief sculpture on the Coatepantli, Tula. A serpent is shown with a head of a human in his jaws. Traces of the original paint are visible. Postclassic period.

Atlantean figures on the top of the Pyramid of Quetzalcoatl, Tula. These sculptures are in sections and then tenoned together. At one time they supported the roof to the Toltec temple. Postclassic period.

The Pyramid of Teopanzolco, built by the Aztecs just prior to the Spanish Conquest, is located in Cuernavaca. Postclassic period.

Carved stone relief on Structure A at Dainzú. Middle Preclassic period.

The round pyramid at Calixtlahuaca has four superimpositions similar in shape and is dedicated to the Wind God, Ehécatl. Postclassic period.

The Aztec site of Malinalco showing part of the main temple with a reconstructed thatch roof. Postclassic period.

Pyramid of the Moon, Teotihuacán. Protoclassic period.

Monument of a warrior found at Tula. The original thin coat of plaster that covered the sculpture is painted a shade of red. Postclassic period. Collection of the Museo Nacional de Antropologia e Historia, Mexico City.

The ball court, Xochicalco. This classic ally shaped ball court has the original stone rings on its vertical walls. Postclassic.

those of the ball courts at Copán and Monte Albán. Both side rings placed in the vertical walls adjoining the benches are uncarved. The opening in the ring is large enough for a human head to pass through. During Aztec times, the openings in ball rings were of many sizes, indicating different types of games played. The size of the solid rubber ball also must have varied according to the type of game played.

During the excavation of the site, a superb stone ball-court marker was discovered, now in the Museum of Anthropology in Mexico City. The marker is pierced in design and has the shape of a macaw's head. The style is similar to ceremonial *hachas* used in conjunction with the ball game—carved in Veracruz during Classic times. This beautifully executed sculpture is a master conception of a parrot in abstraction. Other parrot-head markers are known at the Maya sites of

A parrot-head ball-court marker found near the ball court at Xochical-co. Collection of the Museum of Anthropology in Mexico City. Courtesy The American Museum of Natural History, New York.

Copán and La Unión in Honduras, but their form is more realistic.

Located along the outer sides of the court benches were structures that might have been used by the players as dressing rooms or by the elite to watch the game. There is little indication of these structures today, and their purpose is still unknown. On the south side of the ball court is a stairway for the approach to these structures. With the extensive terracing of hillsides encircling the ball court, it was possible for hundreds of people to see the game easily from these terraced platforms. A similar-shaped ball court constructed in Postclassic times can be seen at the Toltec capital of Tula.

Extending in a westerly direction for several hundred feet is a series of twenty circular platforms, measuring a little over fifteen feet in diameter, which have baffled archaeologists since they were excavated. Raised circular platforms of this type are not known anywhere else in this area. Since they run adjacent to the palace and the causeway from the ball court to the Malinche pyramid, they might have supported columns for a type of structure similar to a peristyle. Such a structure is known at El Tajín. The peristyle would permit a free flow of breeze from the Morelos Valley below and ample shade from the sun for those using the structure. The location of these circular platforms, next to the Palace, suggests that this could have been a reason for such a building here. Archaeologists have also suggested that they may have been altars.

To the east of these columns is a building complex called El Palacio. The structure has been partially restored so that the rooms and side walls are indicated. It may well have been a residence for the ruling families or for priests. It also could have been an administrative center. Many of the rooms are quite small, but some have adjoining courtyards or sunken patios. A sweat bath is located in one section of the palace. From the palace there is a sudden drop in elevation to the valley floor below. During the heat of the day, a light breeze moving over this rugged terrain would be most effective for the people in the palace area.

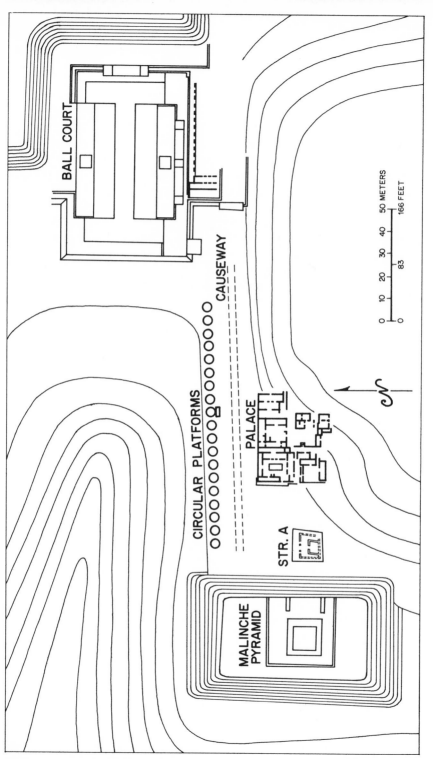

Southwest Section of Ceremonial Center, Xochicalco

El Palacio, Xochicalco. A palace-type structure overlooking the Valley of Morelos. Postclassic.

Just beyond El Palacio are indications of another small structure. Adjoining it is the great pyramid mound known as the Malinche. Little excavation has been done here; however, it would seem the structure must have been of great importance because of its size and superb location overlooking the valley. In the Cortés Palace at Cuernavaca, now a museum, is a stone sculpture of a seated female figure that was found at the Malinche location.

Xochicalco is becoming increasingly important in the history of pre-Columbian civilizations. The site is one that acts as a "bridge" in time, as it straddles both the Late Classic and Postclassic time sequences. The location of the site justifies it as a "crossroads" of diverse cultural developments. Future excavations should reveal more data on who the inhabitants were, the political sphere of the valley, the significance of the trade routes, and the accomplishments of its inhabitants in the sciences.

Teopanzolco

As bleak as it may sound, it is "across the railroad tracks" at Cuernavaca where the traveler may see the Aztec ruins of Teopanzolco. "Place Where the Old Temple Stands" is the romantic Aztec name for the site. From this quiet hilltop is a spectacular view of the present-day city of Cuernavaca and the surrounding country, all a part of the Valley of Morelos. In Aztec times this rich, fertile valley was important because it could supply the quantities of farm produce and other materials demanded for tribute.

From the earliest of times the Valley of Morelos has been a passageway for Indians going from the coastal areas of the south to the Valley of Mexico in the north. This "crossroads" area was influenced by all the major cultural developments throughout the history of Mexico. The area is rich in Preclassic pottery and sculptures that were made locally. In the Classic Period (A.D. 300–900) both the great cities of Teotihuacán and Cholula were to influence this valley. During the Terminal Classic and Early Postclassic periods (A.D. 700–1200) the Valley of Morelos came under the control of Xochicalco. Its history ends with the Aztec take-over of the cities of the valley, followed by the Spanish Conquest.

Today, what remains of the ruins of Teopanzolco covers an area of several acres on a leveled hilltop. The main plaza, so important to the functioning of a ceremonial center, is surrounded by a group of stone platforms of various sizes and shapes. Among these is a round structure, the Temple of Quetzalcoatl dedicated to the God of the Wind. This latter structure has been excavated and, recently, partially restored. The platform construction is of basalt, a volcanic stone found in abundance in the area. Archaeologists found no indication of the superstructure. Facing the east, this small platform is approximately nine feet high and a little over forty-five feet in diameter. The stairway has typically wide Aztec ramps that are unadorned. This temple has many earlier as well as contemporary prototypes. These round, masonry platforms can be seen at Tula, Malinalco, Calixtlahuaca, Zempoala, and Tlatelolco. The style is eclectic, being borrowed from their Toltec predecessors. The quality of the architecture is massive, ponderous, and direct. It is quite possible that painted murals, architectural details such as roof crests, and sculpture added the lighter touch needed to satisfy the cultural demands of that day.

The main pyramid has held the attention of scholars for a number of years. It must have been a very impressive structure at the time the Aztec lords and priests were using it to honor their gods. The pyramid consists of two superimpositions. The last of these two structures was never finished, and, in fact, the building program may have been interrupted by the coming of the Spaniards. However, the main stairway and the side walls to the pyramid are clearly indicated. Should this last superimposition have been completed, it would have extended above and over the first structure, encasing it in the core of the total construction.

The inner pyramid, which today is exposed for the visitor to see, is of particular interest, inasmuch as the partial remains of the side walls of the original two temples on top of the pyramid are still intact. Both chambers of the temples are rectangular and face to the west. The southern temple is larger and was the temple dedicated to the God of War, Huitzilopochtli. The other temple must have been dedicated to Tláloc, God of Water. The four masonry columns here were probably meant to support the roof to the unfinished second superimposition. We can assume the roofs were made of wooden beams

147

*Stairway to the first superimposition of the Aztec pyramid at Teopan-
zolco. Postclassic.*

and thatch or stuccoed stone similar to the roof at Santa Cecilia.
Still remaining on the vertical walls of the temple are serpent
heads of pumice that are tenoned into the well-cut stone structure. Benches run the entire length of the east walls of both
temples. The approach to the temple is by a very steep, double
stairway utilizing ramps for the balustrade that are intermit-
tently broken by vertical cubes with a flat top. The remains of
the original plaster can be seen over much of the building as
well as traces of red color.

At Teopanzolco, as well as at other sites in the Valley of
Morelos, quantites of pottery sherds have been found. Archaeological investigations under the direction of G. C. Vaillant

148

Rear view of the platform supporting the partial temple structures at Teopanzolco. Postclassic.

have given us the classification of these Teopanzolco ceramics. The local ware is called Tlahuica and is typified by a lacquer ware painted in geometric patterns or lines using black and red over a white slip. One of the typical shapes is a simple, hemispherical open bowl. The ware, which has appeared throughout the Valley of Morelos, has some similarities to the Toluca Valley pottery produced by the Matlazincas and is Early Postclassic in date (A.D. 900–1200). Specimens can be seen in the recently restored Palace of Cortés in Cuernavaca.

In the reconstruction of Cortés' Palace, Aztec ruins were found around the foundations. It is quite possible that an extensive archaeological zone exists under the central square of

149

this city. The Cortés Palace was restored in 1974 and contains many archaeological artifacts of interest from various regions of the Valley of Morelos. The palace was constructed for Cortés and used by him after his conquest in Mexico.

V Gulf Coastal Plain

El Tajín

White silken clouds cling to rugged mountain saddles as the descent is made to the Gulf coastal plain. Misty, hot humid air saturates the exotic tropical blossoms along the hillsides and permeates the sugarcane valleys en route to El Tajín. El Tajín is believed to have been the capital of the great classical civilization we refer to as the Veracruz Classic Civilization. This civilization is characterized by regional diversity. Some of the most beautiful stone carvings are on the yokes, *palmas* (palmate stones), and *hachas* (ceremonial axes) used in conjunction with the ball-game ceremonies. In pottery, the cream kaolin ceramics with negative painting decoration are the most popular. And the great number of figurines in clay associated with the Tlalixcoyan-Remojadas-Tierra Blanca area, known as the "laughing faces" or "smiling faces," are noteworthy genre sketches of provincial and ceremonial activities.

The whole area of the Veracruz coast has hardly been touched by archaeologists. Reportedly, there are over five hundred archaeological zones in this vast area, and El Tajín is the only major classic city that has been excavated and partially reconstructed. Even so, El Tajín for the most part is still buried under the countless green mounds stretching into the countryside from the ceremonial center. The site covers approximately 146 acres, extending over the hills and valleys for miles.

A stable source of wealth over the many centuries was essential to the ruling class for the political control of the mass of people needed to construct and maintain a large ceremonial center and city such as El Tajín. This tropical area, exuberant in growth because of abundant rainfall, made year-round crops

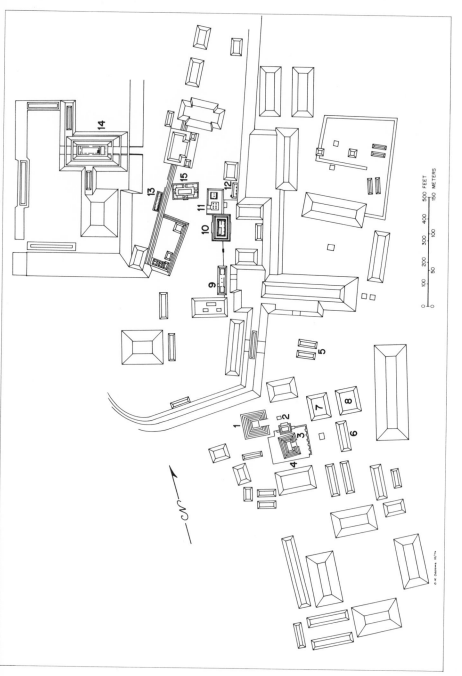

El Tajín

possible. It was the demand from the highlands for cotton, rubber, cacao, coffee, vanilla, and other produce not grown in the Valley of Mexico that gave Veracruz its wealth during Classic times. Many luxury trade items were produced in Veracruz and shipped over a wide area throughout Mesoamerica. For instance, stone *hachas* and yokes have been found throughout the area as far south as Copán. Slate-back mirrors with typical Veracruz designs are known from sites in Guatemala. Veracruz sculptors were to influence stone carving in such classic cities as Cholula and Teotihuacán. Indeed, these cities may have employed craftsmen from the Veracruz area. The large stone monuments recently excavated in the Great Plaza at Cholula are in typical Classic Veracruz style. Markers for the ball courts at Teotihuacán are also in this style. Even the mural paintings at this latter city came under the influence of El Tajín. At Xochicalco the style of the Pyramid of the Plumed Serpent with the flying cornice and dominant *talud* is stylistically related to El Tajín.

The architecture at El Tajín is distinguished by the use of niches on the façades of the pyramids, the use of flying cornices, and the ingenious use of mosaic stone *tableros* to create a play of light and shadow when the sun hits the buildings. El Tajín was no doubt occupied during the Early Classic period, but building activity is only known from A.D. 600. The city reached its height in the Late Classic period, but continued until the twelfth century, at which time it was burned and abandoned.

The ancient ceremonial center of El Tajín, in the hills near Papantla, was unknown until 1785, for it lay buried in a lush jungle growth. Excavation started here in 1945 and was continued in 1954. The ruins are divided into two sections: that area around the Pyramid of the Niches with its associated buildings is known as El Tajín, and the second section on the hillside above the Pyramid of the Niches complex is referred to as El Tajín Chico.

The most important and popularly known structure at El Tajín is the Pyramid of the Niches, constructed in the sixth

Pyramid of the Niches, El Tajín. Classic period.

century. The scale is deceiving, as it looks much larger than the actual measurement—the height to the top of the pyramid is just eighteen meters or sixty feet. With the sanctuary on top, the building could have reached a height of eighty feet. The six receding platforms that form the pyramid consist of a *talud* that supports vertical bands of niches, at one time painted red with blue frames, and a cornice which has overlapping moldings creating a "flying cornice." This design of the platforms is unique to El Tajín. Peculiarly enough, the whole design continues under the stairway. The stairway is attached to the pyramid seemingly as an afterthought, impressive as it may look. Along the length of the stairway are six "altars" that break the pattern of the stairs. Each of these has three niches

154

Balustrades on the stairway to the Pyramid of the Niches are decorated with stylized serpent designs. Classic period.

The plaza area at El Tajín. Structure 3 and 23 are to the left. A ceremonial platform is in the foreground. Classic period.

under it. A balustrade of highly stylized serpents embellishes the stairway. The sanctuary on top of the pyramid is only partially restored and faces the east. The niches on the pyramid, including those under the stairs, total 365, representing the days of the calendar year.

In front of the base of the pyramid are eight square blocks of stone, each with a circular hole in the middle. These were probably used for holding standards. The stairway, approximately thirty-five feet wide, probably functioned as a grandstand for the elite when important ceremonies took place in the small plaza below.

In tunneling into the Pyramid of the Niches, archaeologists discovered another structure under the present pyramid. Its core is constructed of large boulders that rest on a bed of clay. This early structure is believed to have been built in the third century.

At El Tajín there are none of the large plazas so familiar at all the other classic sites. Instead, there is a series of small plazas and courtyards that are adapted to this hilly area by being placed around and between the various structures. In

Structure 5, El Tajín. Indications of red paint are still to be seen on the pyramid surface. Classic period.

front of the Pyramid of the Niches a small platform, with a stairway to the east, might have been used as an altar.

Surrounding the plaza in front of the Pyramid of the Niches is a group of structures very similar in architectural design to the main pyramid, though not as high. Structure 2 is a small platform facing north that is built into the platform of Structure 5. At one time it had two platforms, but only the foundation of the second platform remains today. The stairway is divided by a central ramp that is crowned by three niches and a flying cornice. These niches and cornice continue completely around the four sides of the platform. The *talud* is the dominant element, not only on this structure, but on many of the others at El Tajín. From a design point of view, the *talud* counterbalances the weight of the flying cornice. An earlier substructure with a similar design was discovered inside this platform. Archaeologists have left this exposed so the visitor can see the earlier superimposition.

Structure 5 is to the south of Structure 2, but faces east into another small plaza area. This truncated pyramid rests on a high platform with a single row of niches and flying cornice

The God of Death is depicted in this basalt sculpture located on the platform of Structure 5, El Tajín.

encircling the top. The approach to the top of this first platform is by a double stairway separated by a ramp with niches on each side, and two additional stairways on the north and west sides of the platform. A single stairway with undecorated ramps, facing east, is the approach to the top of the main pyramid. The top platform is a little over thirty feet above the ground level and has a walled enclosure made up of a *tablero* with mosaic fret designs and a flying cornice. A handsomely carved stela is placed on the first platform in front of the main staircase. The sculpture is carved from a block of columnar basalt. According to Tatiana Proskouriakoff, it is of an earlier period than the structure on which it rests today. This imposing sculpture of a grotesque-looking man representing the God of Death is in typical Classic Veracruz style. The double-outlined interlocking meanders in low relief decorate the sculpture. Structure 5, like all structures at El Tajín, was plastered and painted, but little of that remains today. Some of the red paint can be seen on the staircase.

Just to the east of Structure 5 is a small platform in the center of the plaza. Platforms such as this were large enough to be used for religious ceremonies, dances, musicals, or plays. The platform style is similar to the other structures, having a very deep *talud*, a row of niches in the very shallow *tablero*, and a flying cornice. Beyond and directly to the east of this ceremonial platform is Structure 15. Here is a long platform incorporating all the architectural devices used on other structures at El Tajín. However, the length of the platform suggests its use as a secular building, possibly an administrative center, or residential headquarters for the priests.

Two other buildings more recently excavated at El Tajín are Structures 3 and 23 which face the plazas to the south. Both these pyramids are similar, and at one time must have been surmounted by temples. Each structure at El Tajín has a consistent architectural pattern in which the *talud*, *tableros*, and flying cornices dominate. Every structure, however, is slightly different from the other in the handling of tetonic forms. For instance, Structure 3 has seven platforms decorated

159

with very shallow *tableros*, but no niches or frets are incorporated into the platform design. A series of six small platforms with niches and flying cornices break the great staircase from top to bottom. These may have been used for altars or possibly observation areas for the elite to watch activities in the plaza below. On the staircase and along the side of the pyramid can be seen the remains of plaster with blue paint.

Next to Structure 3 is another pyramid of approximately the same size and height that is designated as Structure 23. The platforms are very plain compared to other structures here, having no exterior decoration except paint. The stairway is very different from others here in that there is a wide, central ramp halfway up the pyramid that separates the stairway into two parts. A finial of niches and a flying cornice terminate the ramp. The remainder of the stairway is an uninterrupted single flight to the top platform.

In this section of El Tajín, the lower plaza area, a great number of mounds still have to be excavated before the area can be evaluated completely.

The ball game must have been an extremely important ceremonial happening in its time. At El Tajín there are seven ball courts, only two of which have been excavated. They range in length from approximately 80 to 190 feet. The two excavated courts have vertical walls. No markers or rings have been found. However, beautifully carved bas-reliefs in panels decorate these vertical walls.

Much has been written about how the ball game was played when the Spaniards arrived in the sixteenth century. However, the game may have been played quite differently during Classic times, one thousand years earlier. There is evidence that the ball game was played as early as the Middle Preclassic period (1200–400 B.C.), and that the plain stone yoke may have been used at this time. It would seem that over such a long history there must have been many types of ball games. We know from the wall reliefs that there were "ceremonial" games at which a human may have been sacrificed. There must also have been casual games among the villagers

Stairway to Structure 3 showing six platforms with niches, El Tajín. Classic period.

Stone sculpture showing a ballplayer being dressed for the game. Classic Veracruz. Collection of the Museum of Anthropology in Mexico City.

Stone yoke used for ceremonies in connection with the ball game.
Courtesy The American Museum of Natural History, New York.

and between towns. It is quite possible masonry courts were
not used for some of these games.

It would seem that the ceremonial courts would be within
such great ceremonial centers as El Tajín. The games at these
centers would give the players a chance to wear the ceremonial
paraphernalia associated with the game—the stone yokes,

Southern Ball Court, El Tajín. Pit holes in the center of the court are the result of archaeological excavations. Classic period.

Part of the vertical playing wall of the Southern Ball Court, El Tajín. Classic period.

palmas, and *hachas*. On these stones are lavished magnificent designs attesting to the sheer technical excellence of the sculptors. Some of the handsomest of these stones can be seen in the Museo Nacional de Antropología e Historia in Mexico City and in The American Museum of Natural History in New York City. These stones are symbolic representations of actual padding made of leather, quilting, or raw cotton which protected the player during the game. Since the ball was hard rubber and weighed six or seven pounds, the game was perilous, and the padding softened the blows by the ball or the falls taken by the players. Either before or after the game the ceremonial clothing was worn, and it was then the stone-sculptured pieces were used. Decoration on the stones is highly variable, but most frequently included animals, anthropomorphic figures, human faces, deities, and arabesque-type interlocking designs. Much of the ceremony concerning the game, and how the heavy ceremonial stone carvings were worn, can be best understood by seeing the bas-reliefs on the Southern Ball Court.

The Southern Ball Court is adjacent to Structure 5 and utilizes this platform wall for one side of the court. The court or playing alley is approximately 160 feet long and 60 feet wide, creating quite a long, narrow court. There are six superbly carved bas-relief panels of esoteric ceremonies located at each end and in the center of the vertical walls. These were carved in the Late Classic period, possibly as late as A.D. 900 and are a florescence in low-relief style. Each of the panels is of a different subject. On the northeast corner of the court is a clearly defined scene showing an actual human sacrifice. A seated player is about to be sacrificed. He is held by the arms by one ball player while another player, standing, has a knife pointing to his chest. The three persons are all dressed in ceremonial clothing, including yokes, *hachas*, and palmate stones. To the right of this scene is a chief or ruler witnessing the scene. On the left is the skeletal god of death observing the event. From the upper center of the bas-relief scene descends another god of death. Descending gods, seemingly dropping down from the sky, are noted in sculpture at Classic sites in the

Detail of the stone relief on the Southern Ball Court at El Tajín. An impersonation of a great eagle dominates the mural. Classic period.

Maya area and at Tulúm in the Postclassic period. In this scene at El Tajín the borders have the typical double interlocking curvilinear scrolls that are so much a part of the Classic Veracruz tradition.

Other panels on the Southern Ball Court have magnificent scenes of epic ceremonies not known elsewhere. One of these scenes is on the southwest corner wall of the ball court. A priest dressed in a flamboyant eagle costume sits on the stomach of a person reclining on a bench. On either side are two musicians playing drums and rattles while a "hair-raising" serpent-masked person floats down from the sky in a menacing manner. To the left of the scene is the death god turning his head as though laughing at the event. The four other panels are just as interesting in this story form. Such sculptures as these add

166

Sacrificial scene, Southern Ball Court at El Tajín. Two persons hold the victim to be sacrificed. Classic period.

immeasurably to our knowledge of local ceremonies in regard to the ball game.

The Northern Ball Court is only half as large as the Southern Court, and the bas-reliefs are more decorative than narrative. Intertwined motifs in typical Veracruz Classic style embellish the whole length of these ball-court walls. This ball court is considerably earlier than the Southern Ball Court, believed to have been constructed in the seventh century.

High on a hill above El Tajín is Chico Tajín, that part of the archaeological zone most recently excavated. Chico Tajín is believed to be the secular and administrative center of the city. Much of the ruins here are not excavated, but enough has been restored to make a visit interesting.

At the top of the hill, by proceeding in a northerly direc-

167

The God of Death, a sculpture detail of the sacrificial scene on the Southern Ball Court at El Tajín.

tion, one first encounters Structure K, excavated in 1954. Today little of this structure shows, as a mound of dirt and grass has again grown over it. Just to the north of it is Structure C. Along this pathway even the lowest platforms have finials of the flying cornice that distinguishes El Tajín from all other sites. Structure C is one of the many secular buildings here. Its base platform has a *talud*, and above this rise three platforms in which the *tablero* is executed in a mosaic greco design of stepped meanders and inverted hooks. Another third platform may be the remains of a residential area. The structure has two façades. The one facing the Plaza del Tajín Chico to the west is the most elaborate and has a stairway that continues to the second platform, while the other faces the valley to the east, the Plaza Oriente. The roof of the whole building consists of a single slab of concrete, a typical method of roof construction at El Tajín, and seems to be unique to this area. This mass of concrete, poured in thin layers, was kept light in weight by the use of pumice, wood chips, and pot shards mixed with lime made from powdered seashells and sand. A single block of concrete could span buildings with a fairly sizable roof. On Structure C the span is approximately 495 square feet. The exterior surface of the building was painted blue, but the niches that act as fenestration for the platforms were painted red. Roof combs were used on some structures at El Tajín, and on Structure C are the remains of a roof comb in which the decorative motif is the inverted hook within niches.

Adjacent to Structure C is Structure B, another residential building that is not too dissimilar in architectural style. The pyramid rises on four platforms, and superstructures are placed on the top platform. The large *tableros* on the façade are plain, and in this way relate to the style of those on Structure 23 in the valley below Chico Tajín.

Just to the east is Structure D, quite a different type of structure from any encountered here so far. This low platform has a deep *talud* that is totally covered with an unusually large lozenge design. The top of the platform supported a sanctuary

Structure C at Chico Tajín is believed to have been one of the administrative buildings at El Tajín. Classic period.

Detail of the façade of Structure C showing the "flying cornice," El
Tajín. Classic period.

Structure D, Chico Tajín. A decoration of a large lozenge design is unusual. Classic period.

open to the east by a porticoed chamber that was supported by three columns. The view from this sanctuary gives a sweeping panorama of the lush, green valley below. Much of the structure now lies in ruin.

Structure A at Chico Tajín is possibly the most important building here that is restored. This structure and Structures B and C probably date from the ninth century. Structure A faces the Plaza de Tajín Chico. On this southern side the interior of the building is reached by a stairway with a corbelled vault, quite a rare occurrence outside the Maya area. The structure is on a platform that supports an outer wall which has rooms on all four corners. Between these rooms and a large central chamber is a passageway encircling the whole interior of the building. The exterior and interior of the building are broken into a series of panels with all the familiar meander designs used at

171

Interior of Structure A at Chico Tajín showing carving in deep relief. Classic period.

El Tajín. One of the new leitmotifs in the interior of the building is that of a swastika bas-relief on a series of lower panels. Much of the original plaster and polychrome paint remains on Structure A. Some of the panels were painted in murals, but only swatches of the paint remain today.

There are many superimpositions, reconstructions, and alterations in the buildings at El Tajín. This should be expected because of the very long history of construction here. One of the most interesting buildings is a very small platform just to the west of Structure A. Originally the structure was in the architectural form of peristyles. A number of columns in two rows held up a roof with a flying cornice. The structure was open to the breeze in true pergola style. Later in the history of El Tajín this structure was enclosed with walls, creating a long room with four doors. The use of a peristyle-type structure

172

is rare in Mesoamerican history. The Great Vestibule at Tula is the closest evidence we have of this style of architecture.

On the hill above Structure Q is the Building of the Columns resting on a natural hilltop that was leveled for the structure and the adjoining plaza and associated buildings. It is the largest of all the buildings at El Tajín, but, unfortunately, it has not been restored. The Building of the Columns has a large plaza west and south that is surrounded by other buildings still visible only as mounds, the largest of these being the Building of the Tunnels. The stairway to the Building of the Columns is on four platforms, and it must have been extremely impressive from the administrative center below. However, today there is nothing restored, and it is in a ruined condition. The base of the façade is decorated in a very bold Greek cross design. Balustrades to the stairway are embellished with a vertebrae motif. Six columns were used to support a portico on a platform in front of the stairway to the façade. These columns were constructed of stone drums covered with sculpture in low relief. Here we can see deities, warriors, and priests as well as epic scenes and calendar glyphs. Because of vandalism, some of these great drums have been removed to the little museum area at the entrance to the archaeological zone.

Inside the Building of the Columns, believed to have been built during the eleventh century, was an open patio, surrounded by a bench and a series of chambers. Today the whole structure is a pile of rubble with little indication of the grandeur it once displayed.

There is a great need for much more excavation at El Tajín, and in the Veracruz area in general, before there can be a clear chronology and a better understanding of the Classic Veracruz cultural development. Manifestation of this style is best seen in the carved stones in association with the ball game. However, the clay figurines and slate mirrors typify other regional aspects of the Classic Veracruz style.

One of the most alluring groups of sculptured objects to come to light in Veracruz in recent years is the famous laughing figurines. The facial expression is one of contagious happi-

Laughing boy figurine, Remojadas, Veracruz, typical of the ceramic figurines made during the Classic period. Private collection.

174

Slate mirror back carved in low relief, warrior with beard. Veracruz Classic period. Courtesy The American Museum of Natural History.

ness with the whole face smiling from pure joy. These figurines, along with many others, were found in great numbers at Remojadas and Tenenexpan. The classic Remojadas clay sculpture is not only a vigorous art expression of the time, but the many genre sculptures give us an insight into the daily activities and other concerns of the people. Some of the clay figurines have whistles on the back, indicating that they may have been used in some type of processional, possibly by children.

Another important type of sculpture comprises the circular slate mirror-backs carved in elaborate relief of deities or

175

personages in interlocking scroll designs. The reflective surfaces are made up of thin mosaic pyrite or hemetite stones
superbly fitted together and then polished. These mirrors have
holes on the sides, indicating they may have been worn around
the neck.

The Classic period continued much later in Veracruz than
in any other region in Mesoamerica. Its isolation was part of
the reason for this long, uninterrupted history of cultural
development. However, like all civilizations, it, too, collapsed
from pressures within and without the area. During the last
two centuries, influence from the Mixtec and Toltec areas was
being felt at El Tajín. A decadance was already creeping into
the art and architectural forms, and not much later the region
was to be abandoned and recaptured by the jungle until the
present time.

Zempoala

As dawn unfolds the regularity of another humid, hot day
along the Veracruz coast, the village people slowly move into a
pattern of activities that has changed little over the centuries.
Veracruz has been remote enough from the rest of Mexico to
preserve many of its regional traditions. However, the discovery
of oil has now created a rather unpleasant smell from the
countless flames that burn off excess gases, and old customs
are giving way to some modern ideas. Along the highway can
be seen the sugarcane plantations, the orchid plant that gives
us our vanilla bean, and cacao. Such luxury items as these
latter two have long been featured in trade goods to the Mexican plateau.

Zempoala, an Indian name meaning "abundance of
water," is approximately forty miles north of the city of Veracruz just a short distance off the main coastal highway. Zempoala is the name of the present-day village as well as the name
of the adjacent ruins. In fact, one of the many pyramids is isolated in part of the village. Ancient monuments and structures
are not unusual in the villagers' gardens or courtyards.

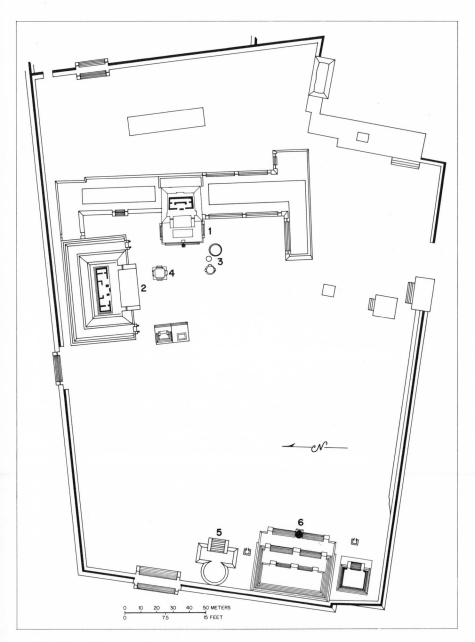

Section of Zempoala (After J. García Payón)

Zempoala was well known to Hernando Cortés and his soldiers. Spanish chronicles record a population of thirty thousand. Bernal Díaz records that the high polish of the architectural structures at first fooled his soldiers, who thought that the buildings were plated with silver. Zempoala was built both as a ceremonial center and as a defense against the Aztecs, who eventually conquered the city. The city had eleven defense systems of various types, and each was enclosed by a defense wall nearly four feet high. Only one of these defense systems has been excavated and partially restored. The rest of the systems are scattered in the village and in corn fields far into the distant landscape.

The irrigation system was especially well planned so that water could be distributed throughout the coastal plain. The ceremonial center of Zempoala was well-engineered in terms of water supply and drainage. Subterranean pipes carried water to all parts of the ancient city. Flooding was an especially acute problem, and many of the walls were built to protect the city from floods. The merlons noted on the pyramids today were the same type of merlons used as a decorative device for the top of the wall enclosures. Because of the many rivers coming down from the mountains, riverbed boulders or water-worn stones were most important for the construction of the city. These beautiful, smooth, ovoid stones were used for wall construction, being cemented together with sand and lime made from seashells. The wall was then smoothed over with plaster and painted in red and yellow colors. One of the earliest uses of riverbed stones for construction is at Cuicuilco, a Late Preclassic city approximately fifteen miles from Mexico City. At Cuicuilco the smooth riverbed stones were set in clay and faced with a plaster of clay and painted red.

Many of the structures at Zempoala face east to the rising sun. This is true of the Temple of the Wind God and the Grand Pyramid, and it is not unusual for ceremonial centers along the Gulf Coast. Because of the mountain ranges to the west, the setting sun does not have the significance that it did to peoples living on the Mexican plateau. Most of the structures at Zem-

The Great Plaza at Zempoala, Las Chimeneas in the distance. Post-classic.

poala were religious, administrative, or residential, but today we see only the platforms of these structures. According to the chronicles, the major buildings on the platforms were of palms.

Architecture at Zempoala is an expression of Aztec and Totonac cultures. Here we can see temples similar to those at Tenochtitlán, some rectangular and others circular in form. The distinctive quality about Zempoala architecture is the abundant use of toothed merlons on the top of walls, platforms, and various types of enclosures. These merlons are all similar in design, being much like the stepped fret design used by the Mixtec at Mitla. Because of the lack of large stones, sculpture was mainly limited to cement or ceramics.

Explorations at Zempoala started as early as 1891 by the Comisión Científica Exploradora. In 1902 further study of the area was carried out by Jesse Walter Jenkins of the Smithsonian Institution. After 1939 all investigation has been un-

Pyramid at Zempoala showing the use of riverbed stones for construction. Postclassic.

dertaken by the Instituto Nacional de Antropologia e Historia.

The most impressive of the structures at Zempoala is the Templo Mayor (Major Temple) at the extreme north side of the Great Plaza. Construction materials were obtained from local sources. Most structures at Zempoala have a core of adobe or sand and soil. The pyramid was then faced with a series of riverbed stones in from two to six rows that were cemented together. Originally this base was plastered so that the stones did not show, and the structure was painted. With the typical moisture along the coast and the abundant rainfall, most of the cement plaster has disappeared, leaving the naked beauty of the ovoid stones exposed. Most of the structures at Zempoala have had many additions and superimpositions over the years.

The Templo Mayor went through a period of four major reconstructions.

The pyramid rests on a large masonry terrace that is reached by two small lateral staircases on either side of the grand staircase that faces south. A low wall decorated with merlons encloses the platform. At one time four urns, possibly for a lighted flame were situated on the two approaches to the terrace. The pyramid rises on thirteen platforms to a height of approximately thirty-five feet, and is approached by a great staircase ninety feet wide bordered by ramps. The top platform is also walled and decorated with merlons. The partial remains of a sanctuary with three rooms is still visible. The largest room, in the center, has a raised platform that may have been used as an altar. In its time the Templo Mayor, in brilliant color, must have been an impressive structure.

Adjacent and to the west of the Templo Mayor is a structure called Las Chimeneas (The Chimneys). The name is taken from the circular hollow columns on the platform in front of the stairway. These were at one time reinforced with a wooden core, but over the years weathering rotted the core, leaving a hollow masonry construction. In 1519, Cortés, his men, and fifteen horses were lodged in this section of Zempoala. It was here that plans were laid for the expedition to meet Moctezuma. Fortunately for Cortés, the Totonac Indians of this region were only too glad to join forces and stage an uprising against the Aztecs, as their tribute to them was unusually large. The Aztecs had also taken over six thousand captives from the conquest to be sacrificed at their capital. The fierce Totonacs were not to forget their loss of pride in that war. By joining forces with the Spaniards, they presented a frightening power block to Moctezuma and his armies.

Las Chimeneas was a temple-pyramid erected on a long platform in the shape of a capital "E" that runs north and south to the Great Plaza. The pyramid has seven platforms, the first one having been covered when the extensive terrace was constructed on either side. The stairway is bordered by two plain ramps. Although there is no temple on top of this pyra-

Platform for the temple to the Wind God, Ehécatl, Zempoala.

mid today, at one time it had a two-room structure with two doorways. Stepped-fret merlons were placed as finials around the three sides of the top platform.

Bordering the east side of the Great Plaza is the temple to the Wind God, the Great Pyramid, and another temple structure. The Great Pyramid faces the east and rises from a series of three platforms to a height of twenty-five feet. This double stairway, bordered by ramps, is quite typical of the architectural style used by both the Toltecs and the Aztecs during the Postclassic period (A.D. 900–1520). On the first platform in the center of the stairway is a firebox for a lighted flame. As on the top platforms of other structures at Zempoala, the wall of merlons is present also on the Great Pyramid. This structure is thought to have been the temple dedicated to the Sun God.

Adjacent to the Great Pyramid is believed to be the temple to the Wind God, Ehécatl. Circular temples during Postclassic times are noted at Tula, Calixtlahuaca, Malinalco, Teopanzolco, Tlatelolco, and Tenochtitlán. We know from the sculpture carved in the living rock at Malinalco that this temple was dedicated to the Order of the Eagles and Jaguars. At Calixtla-

182

Circular altar in the Great Plaza, Zempoala. Postclassic.

huaca the circular structure was dedicated to Ehécatl, the Wind God, as his statue of clay was found in the interior of one of the superimpositions. At Tenochtitlán one of the circular temples was dedicated to the Earth Goddess, Coatlicue. At Zempoala we can only assume that the temple is dedicated to the Wind God because of its shape. At the front of this circular structure is a large rectangular platform that leads to a stairway with ramps facing the Great Plaza to the East. These two rooms are on a singular pyramid base constructed of five platforms. Beneath this platform is an earlier superimposition with four platforms.

In the Great Plaza is a series of altars or *adoratorios*, some rectangular or square, two others circular, located to the west of Las Chimeneas. On the latter is noted a repeat of the decorative merlon found on other structures at Zempoala.

Even though Zempoala was a great distance from the Aztec capital and the Totonacs who lived here disliked Aztec control, it would seem the area was infused by Aztec religion, architecture, and minor crafts. Even the island, Isla de los Sacrificios in the Gulf of Mexico, was very much a part of the Aztec empire. Spanish chronicles describe the island as an important Aztec religious ceremonial center where the sacrifice of humans was witnessed. Moctezuma's plans to include Guatemala and the Caribbean islands as a part of his empire were thwarted by the Spanish *conquistadores*. Had Cortés and his warriors not arrived in Mexico at the time they did, quite a different history of this last all-Indian civilization might have been written.

VI Valley of Oaxaca

Monte Albán

In the southern highlands of Mexico is a very fertile, rich valley that became one of the cradles for a great civilization lasting well over one thousand years. The Valley of Oaxaca has been a passageway for movements of people migrating from the Plateau of Mexico to the Isthmus of Tehuantepec, Chiapas, and the Maya areas along the Pacific Slope, the Guatemala Highlands, and into the Petén. Semitropical, at an elevation of five thousand feet, the valley contains many types of microenvironments. Part of the region is very arid, other areas are swamps, but much of the land supports agricultural pursuits. It is believed that at one time the Valley of Oaxaca had a heavier rainfall and was more fertile than at present. But with over four thousand years of agriculture, the natural vegetation of the valley has been destroyed, erosion has been disastrous, and the land is now more arid. There is some indication of terracing and irrigation of the land in Late Preclassic times (400 B.C.–A.D. 1), utilizing it to the fullest extent, but little remains of this agricultural system today. Much of the land is overgrown with cactus and oak, and at the higher altitudes pine and oak forests are found.

Toward the end of Early Preclassic times (2000–1200 B.C.) a brisk trade in crafted goods was already well under way in the Valley of Oaxaca. Pearls, shells from the Pacific coast, and other natural objects were being made into ornaments. Artisans were working with mica and iron ores such as magnetite and ilmenite, fashioning them into mirrors. These trade goods could be used as part of an exchange system when

185

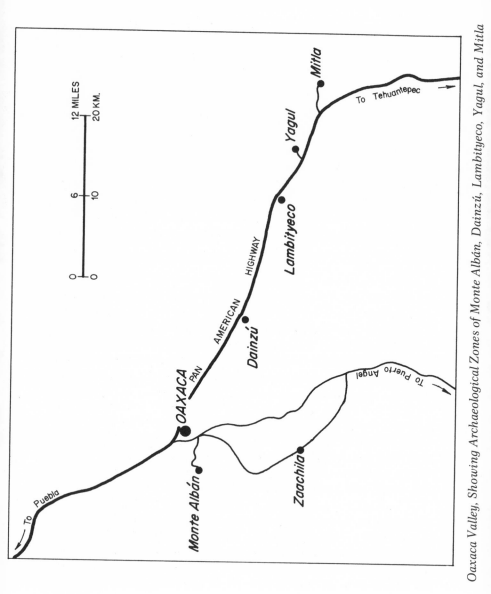

Oaxaca Valley, Showing Archaeological Zones of Monte Albán, Dainzú, Lambityeco, Yagul, and Mitla

The Main Plaza and part of the ceremonial center of Monte Albán.

erratic weather caused crop failures. The need for trade and the specialization of artisans were instrumental in laying the foundation for cultural development.

During Middle to Late Preclassic times (1200 B.C.–A.D. 1) a greater number of villages appeared in the valley as the population increased. Social status is noted by the variety of houses in the community centers. The elite had houses raised on platforms and built of adobe brick and then plastered and painted. Dramatically impressive ceremonial and civic centers were being constructed on hilltops and these structures attested to the skills of the architects and sculptors of the time. Such a site is Monte Albán, and it is only one of over two hundred ancient city centers in the Valley of Oaxaca. Of these, travelers will be particularly interested in Zaachila, Mitla, Dainzú, Yagul, and Lambityeco, all easily accessible by car.

Monte Albán ("White Mountain") rests majestically on the leveled-off mountaintop high above the cares of the weary people working in the valley below. One of the great panoramic views of distant green valleys and hazy blue-colored mountains is to be seen from this famous archaeological site. On this

187

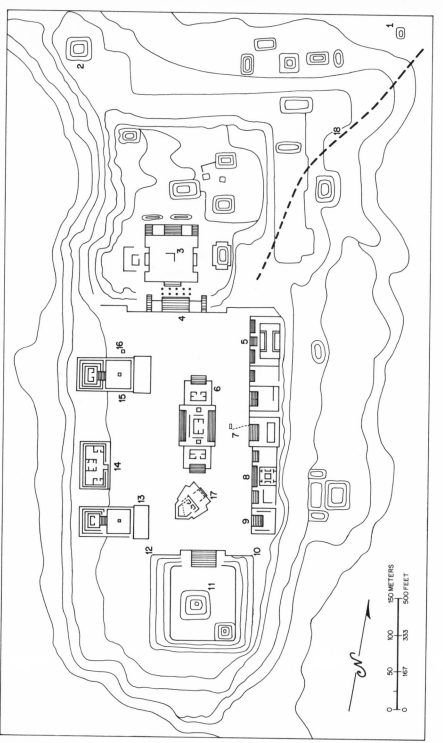

Monte Albán (After Paddock)

hilltop have been found some of the richest tomb treasures in America. There are over 150 tombs located here, burial grounds for nearly two thousand years, and some of them are painted with brilliant murals.

A climb to the top of the Southern Platform at one end of the Great Plaza reveals the complexity of the structures to be encountered. Here are enormous courtyards, pyramids of great temples, platforms of palaces, foundations of innumerable smaller structures, a restored ball court, and many dozens of mounds not yet excavated.

Five distinct epochs have been designated for the time sequence at Monte Albán, which span the years from 800 B.C. to A.D. 1500. They are designated as:

Monte Albán I (800–400 B.C.)
Monte Albán II (400 B.C.–A.D. 1)
Transitional Period (A.D. 1–300)
Monte Albán III A (A.D. 300–900)
Monte Albán III B (A.D. 600–900)
Monte Albán IV (A.D. 900–1520)

Monte Albán III A and B are the Early and Late Classic phase, and the latter is a little more elaborate than the former. This style change is noted mostly in the ceramics. With Monte Albán IV there is an obvious decline in quality and craftsmanship. Most of the latter part of this period is really Mixtec rather than Zapotec and is sometimes distinguished as Monte Albán V. The Mixtecs entered the valley after Monte Albán was abandoned and established an influence over a vast area. They were not great architects, but they were excellent craftsmen, creating superb jewelry not equaled in the Americas up to this time. Some of their treasures have been found in older Zapotec tombs. The Zapotecs are believed to have occupied the Valley of Oaxaca as far back as 250 B.C., and their descendants are still living in the valley today.

When the earliest structures were occupied at Monte Albán (Monte Albán I — 800–400 B.C.) in Preclassic times, there were several other important cultural areas that had attained a prom-

189

inent place in Mesoamerican history as well. In the Plateau of Mexico the sites of Copilco, Ticoman, Tlatelolco, and Zacatenco were active; the Olmec civilization was coming to a close on the Gulf coastal plain; Izapa was busily occupied in the development of a transitional style of sculpture that was to have its fruition in Late Preclassic times; the earliest beginnings of the Maya civilization were just in the process of developing; and, on the coast of Yucatán, Dzibilchaltún was an active coastal trading center. There were also many other areas that were undergoing cultural change.

At Monte Albán and nearby Monte Negro to the north, the period of Monte Albán I reflects the cultural contact with the Olmec area in particular. This was especially true in jade carving and some of the sculptures. It would seem, however, that the people occupying Monte Albán at that time were by far better architects, and were certainly more advanced in their system of writing, mathematics, and calendrics, than the Olmecs to the east. This can readily be seen in the *Danzante* structure and in the carvings of glyphs on stones adjacent to that area. The glyphs are much more numerous and have a greater variety of meanings than at La Venta and other Olmec sites. Further, Monte Albán use of bars and dots (standing for numerals 5 and 1) set a pattern in numerical notation for future civilizations. There is every indication of heavy trade between Monte Albán and the Olmec region, where each had luxury items the other desired. However, in religion, the Olmecs seemingly had fewer deities (the jaguar and serpent cults being present). According to Ignacio Bernal, at Monte Albán at least ten deities, all male, have been identified so far.

The *Danzante* structure located in the southwest area of the Great Plaza represents the initial stage of building at Monte Albán. The structure, erected on bedrock, was buried under a building of the Late Classic period. Only partially revealed, the *Danzante* building is constructed of very large, flat flagstones on vertical walls that are incised with the so-called *Danzante* figures in association with glyphs and numerals. The structure is believed to be of the seventh century B.C.,

Danzante *stone carvings, Monte Albán I. Glyphs are on the nude figure and the space surrounding him. The stone carving to the right is a series of glyphs.*

and it may be the earliest structure here. Structures of the same period are still buried in the core of other buildings under the north platform or have been destroyed for later structures. However, some tombs of this early period remain. It is believed that the platform on the *Danzante* building had a superstructure of wood and thatch, most likely a temple. Even at this time a plastered lime floor was in use, one of the earliest known. The architecture of this early culture was more sophisticated than any other of that time in Mesoamerica.

We do not know the precise meaning of the incised carving on the sculptured stones known as the *Danzantes*. These nude male figures have been interpreted as dancers by some historians because the style suggests a definite lilting movement

191

of the body, thus the "dancer." They have also been interpreted as dead captives because of the closed eyes and the many figures that have the penis removed, replaced by a decorative scroll that may represent hairs. Since some of the figures are lying down, others are crawling or swimming, and a few in other positions, it is possible that these stone reliefs were assembled as a narrative scene related to one of the religious ceremonies of the time. There are 140 of these figures known at Monte Albán. The head is always in profile, eyes are closed and puffy, mouth open, nose broad and acquiline, and the legs bent. Today most of these large stones are located at the *Danzante* structure. However, many others are scattered throughout the archaeological zone, some having been reused during Classic time.

The figures are in two styles, suggesting an earlier and later time phase. In the earlier style there is no differentiation between the fingers and toes except for the big toe and thumb. The later style shows the incising deeper in the stone; the figures are more slender and limbs are longer; the mouth not as large and the teeth are showing. At this time we see face paint or tattooing. On many of the stone carvings are accompanying glyphs. The glyphs used here are distinctive from those in other regions in Mesoamerica. To date, the most elaborate system of writing in Middle Preclassic times was at Monte Albán. The *Danzante* figures are believed to have been carved about 700 B.C.

The sculpture of this period is especially interesting to travelers who have been to Dainzú, a short distance from Mitla. The Dainzú structure of similar cut stone with incised male figures is of approximately the same period. The Dainzú figures, however, are mostly ball players. In South America, in the north central coastal desert region of Peru, are similar incised carvings at the archaeological site of Cerro Sechín. This site, recently restored, is believed to be approximately the same period as the carvings at Monte Albán and Dainzú.

The Monte Albán II epoch (400 B.C.–A.D. 1) is a gradual transitional stage from Monte Albán I. Besides Monte Albán

Building J, the Observatory, Monte Albán II. The South Platform is in the distance.

there are over twenty other known sites of this period in the Valley of Oaxaca. Lines of communication must have been well established throughout the valley. Even as far south as the site of Chiapa de Corzo are many similarities with this period of Monte Albán. Since there are no indications of fortifications throughout the whole history of Monte Albán, we can assume this particular area of Mexico lived in comparative harmony with other cultural areas. Monte Albán II saw the leveling and paving of the Great Plaza and the construction of Building J. The task must have been enormous, since this location was on the top of a mountain. Building J has vertical side walls of large slab stones similar to Monte Albán I, and some of these stones are incised with sculptural elements and glyphs. Many of the sculptures are similar, consisting of a central element which stands for a hill or place name with an additional glyph or design above. Underneath these elements is an inverted head. Below it may be additional numerical glyphs. Alfonso Caso suggests that these heads represent de-

193

Glyphs on the exterior walls of the Observatory, Monte Albán II.

194

feated kings from the various regional city-states. The glyphs may refer to the kings' names or the places where they originated. There are about forty glyphic inscriptions of this type on the observatory and on other stones scattered on the ground in the adjacent region.

Building J is also called the Observatory. The building is in the shape of a massive arrowhead with the main stairway approached from the northeast side. Wide balustrades on the sides of the stairway still have indications of plaster. Cutting through the length of the structure from one end to the other is an open passageway which has a roof that is vaulted. This is accomplished by placing long, rectangular stones diagonally against each other to shape the roof. The corbel arch is rare outside the Maya area, but it can be seen in Structure A at El Tajín, in a vaulted tomb near Oztotitlan, Guerrero, and in some of the burial chambers at Monte Albán. However, the Mayas, so famous for their corbel arches, used a completely different and most sophisticated construction. Building J is believed to have had at one time a sanctuary on top made of adobe with a thatch roof. Within the Building J structure are many superimpositions that can be seen from the top of the platform.

A similar structure to this has been found at the nearby site of Caballito Blanco. These building platforms in the arrow shape have been investigated recently for astronomical alignments. At both sites there are indications of a solar alignment in the front of the structures, while the arrow of these platforms point to bright stars.

The first ball court appears at Monte Albán at this time. At Izapa there is another ball court of this period, and more research may reveal others. We do know that as early as the Middle Preclassic period (1200–400 B.C.) the ball game was played, as figurines in clay at Tlatelolco show players with the ball in their hands. Also the Dainzú sculptures depict the ball players in action.

Another monument of Monte Albán II period is Stela 18, located near Structure IV. This is a simple rectangular shaft

195

South entrance to an interior passage on Building J, Monte Albán II.

Stela 18 located near System 4, Monte Albán II. Glyps panels are visible on the east facing.

approximately seventeen feet high that is partially restored. There are lightly incised glyphs on the east facing hardly visible today. Pottery as well as other artifacts of this period shows some Maya influence. The style of the ceramic funerary urns was set at this time: that is, the seated figure of a deity in a frontal position with crossed legs and hands resting on the knees. Another skill of the artisans of the time was jade carving. The unusual high polish on jade was a goal of the Olmecs as well as jade craftsmen at Monte Albán. A most striking deep-green jade mosaic mask of the Bat God composed of twenty-five pieces of jade was found in the Great Plaza at Monte Albán, and this, too, is of the Monte Albán II period. This glistening jade masterpiece can be seen today in the Museo Nacional de Antropologia e Historia in Mexico City.

The intense building program during Monte Albán II, the refinement in the arts, and the multiplication of deities (fifteen known for this time—one a female) suggest a theocratic type of government ruled by chieftains or priests controlling a structured society with clearly defined class distinctions. These were a people who looked beyond their own valley for cultural development. Not only were they dependent on the Gulf Coast for many of their raw materials and luxury products, but there is every indication that the Izapas and Mayas were influencing them stylistically in their art forms.

Most of the visible structures that can be seen today at Monte Albán were constructed during the Classic period known as Monte Albán III A and B (A.D. 300–900). Many of these were built over earlier structures. There is no sharp definition of architectural style from Monte Albán III A to Monte Albán III B. It is in the sculpture and especially the great funerary urns that the style changes from one of simplicity to elaborateness. This was the period when the powerful civilization of Teotihuacán highly influenced styles in architecture, ceramics, sculpture, and mural painting, not only at Monte Albán but throughout most of Mesoamerica. Even the Mayas were to come under this influence. It was also a time when Monte Albán reached its peak in population, covering all the surrounding hillsides and encompassing an area of some fifteen square miles.

The leitmotif in architectural decoration is a variation of the *talud* and *tablero,* popularly used during Classic times to lend decoration to the exterior walls of buildings. This architectural style at Monte Albán is distinctive because of the "open" *tablero* instead of the rectangular "closed" frame so popular at Teotihuacán. This new tetonic form was one of robust, massive elements in which monumental structures were created with harmonizing, refined classic lines that were synthesized into a style unique to Monte Albán.

The funeral chambers were now much more elaborate, and many were painted with murals, highly influenced by the style at Teotihuacán—formalized and conventionalized with much iconographic detail of a religious nature. Funerary urns reached the peak of their style with Monte Albán III, with many more deities now represented on the urns than in the previous epoch. These urns were placed in tombs as offerings to the gods, or they may have represented protective deities who watched over the dead. Although sometimes referred to as *incensarios,* no trace of ash or smoke is indicated on the urns to suggest such use. Trade items, especially jade, have been found with Monte Albán III tombs that are obviously in both Classic Maya and Classic Teotihuacán style.

On approaching the Great Plaza, the traveler is first impressed by the length of the ceremonial center, the formality of the plan, and the number of structures visible in a sweeping glance. One of the most imposing platforms here is that of the North Platform and the adjacent sunken courtyards to the north. It is here that a continuous building program was carried on from Preclassic times. There are many earlier structures buried under the present platform, which is considered Monte Albán III A (Early Classic). The platform is approached by a grand staircase 231 feet wide. Tremendous ramps, 39 feet wide, run parallel to the stairway, and these ramps may well be the widest ever constructed in Mesoamerica. At the top are the remains of twelve circular masonry pillars, seven feet

North Platform, Monte Albán. There are many superimpositions here. The open doorway is to a chamber containing reliefs from Monte Albán I times.

in diameter, indicating that a great portico was attached to the front of the building. The portico was so arranged that a triumphant arch with three spacious openings led into the inner chambers. At the foot of the central stairway is a single stela carved with glyphs on four sides, those on the north being best preserved. The North Platform must surely have been one of the most impressive encountered in Early Classic times.

To the north of the main structure are innumerable other buildings still unexcavated today. Here one can see the many courtyards, some having small altars or shrines in the center. This style of courtyard is very similar to the courtyards at Teotihuacán. The façade of the North Platform has rounded corners not found on other structures at Monte Albán. There is a small entrance room on the east side of the stairway to

Stone relief of a man impersonating a jaguar, a carving incorporated in the building of the North Platform, Monte Albán I.

the North Platform which contains sculptures from Monte Albán I that were incorporated into this structure at an earlier time than the existing building. Here one can again see the *danzante*-style figures. One is of particular importance as it depicts a man crawling on his hands and knees, and it may have been part of a larger group of sculptures that represented a ceremonial scene in which the jaguar was the central cult figure. Jaguars were commonly depicted in pottery during the Late Preclassic and Classic epochs.

The ball court is diagonally to the east of the North Platform. It is a Classic ball court in the form of a capital "I" with a stairway at either end for the players. In two of the diagonal corners is a niche which could have been used for the placement of a deity for each team. It may also have been a place for libations or even a container for fresh water to soothe the

Ball court, Monte Albán III. Earlier ball courts were found under this structure.

sweating bodies of the players. (Similar niches can be seen in an unrestored ball court adjacent to Tomb 105). The sloping side walls, that look like miniature bleachers, were actually plastered over into a flat *talud* and used as part of the playing area for the game. No rings (to pass the ball through) were used in the courts of this time. However, the remains of a central marker can be seen in the middle of the playing alley. This structure was enlarged at different times, but little remains of the earlier construction. The present structure was probably erected during Monte Albán III B. Two plaques, now removed, were located on the east sloping wall, one with the Zapotec date 8.E.8. Turquoise. The game could be watched by the elite or the populace from the four chambers that were at one time located above the sides of the court or from the ends of the court.

To the south of the ball court is a series of platforms that at one time may have been used as palaces for the priests or

Platforms for palace-type structures on the east side of the Main Plaza, Monte Albán III.

rulers. Many superimpositions can be noted in the stairways and in the interior of the structures. The buildings are all quite similar in architectural style, in which the broad stairways have very wide ramps broken by vertical cubes decorated with the "open" *tablero*. In the third structure, going south, there is an unusual feature not encountered elsewhere at Monte Albán. A cleverly planned tunnel goes underground from the interior of this structure to the central platform in the middle of the Great Plaza, no doubt for the convenience of the priests. Today one may wish to crawl through this small tunnel to see how it is constructed. At the halfway point is an exit where an *adoratorio* is located. The tunnel is closed beyond this point. One of the last structures (to the south) in this group has the remains of dwelling rooms surrounding an open court enclosed by a wall, and a cruciform burial chamber in the center of the

The Central Platform, Structure H, dominates the Main Plaza, Monte Albán III.

Cruciform burial chamber located on the top of System M, Monte Albán III.

court. A similar burial chamber is found on the top platform of the *Danzante* structure. The superimposition over the *Danzante* structure is from Monte Albán III B period.

In the center of the Great Plaza is the Central Pyramid Complex (Structure H) which at one time was a single platform for three temple structures. Stairways are on all four sides of the platform, with the major stairways facing east and west. Only the east stairways are restored. This surely must have been the most holy of all the structures at Monte Albán.

To the south of Structure H and beyond Building J is the South Platform, an impressively high structure with a grand staircase, a striking feature of most platforms at Monte Albán. This particular stairway, 132 feet wide, leads to the top platform 82 feet high which at one time held two small temples. Because of its height, the structure dominates the area and offers a magnificent view of the valley below. From here one can see the many unexcavated mounds along pathways running approximately a mile to the south. At the base of the northeast corner of the platform is a group of four stelae from Period I, one being a stone copy of the original. One is an unusual stela of a person impersonating an opossum. These stelae are covered with a most interesting group of glyphs and should be examined carefully. There are two additional stelae on the west façade. The larger of these is a prisoner whose hands are tied behind his back. Another single stela is just a few yards west of the South Platform, also decorated with a figure in Monte Albán I style.

Along the west side of the Great Plaza is the *Danzante* structure (already described) and two additional large structures, very similar in style, known as System M and System 4. These were probably built during the Late Classic time (Monte Albán III B), and have a similar pattern of architecture to most of the other structures found here. Only the platforms are in existence today. Here the platforms have great central stairways flanked by wide balustrades in the form of ramps, and the typical "open" panels or *tableros* on the ramps and

Stone relief of a man impersonating an opossum with his hands tied behind his back, located on the north side of the South Platform, Monte Albán III.

the side wall of the pyramid. These buildings, like all buildings at Monte Albán, were plastered and painted. Red was one of the most popular colors. Here, as elsewhere, the sculptures were also plastered and painted. In front of both structures are walled-in patios built at a later time so as to align them with the other structures running north to south. In the center of the patio of System 4 and System M is a small altar. To the north of System 4 is Stela 18, already described. A tunnel to the north side of System 4 leads to an inner superimposition which is believed to have been constructed during Monte Albán II. At Monte Albán there are many earlier structures under the ones visible today. This Monte Albán II structure has a platform similar to the *Danzante* building, but there are no carved stones here.

The burial chambers in the Northern Cemetery at Monte Albán are some of the most interesting in Mesoamerica. This area is just north of the North Platform and can be reached by a series of paths that go to the famous tombs to be found here. The area had been used as a burial place since the time of Monte Albán I, although most of the tombs are of a later date. Tombs 104 and 7 are the best known. Tomb 105, on an adjacent hillside a quarter of a mile to the northeast, is equally noted for its architecture and murals.

A pathway going northwest from the North Platform leads to Tomb 104, a burial chamber constructed for an important person during Late Classic times. The style of the tombs of this period and their superstructures reached a florescence not equaled elsewhere. A cornice with several moldings runs the length of the façade. The molded cornice of Tomb 104 frames a niche above the crypt entrance, where a ceramic figure of the rain god, Cocijo has been placed. A single slab of stone inscribed with glyphs is used for the door to the tomb. Inside the chamber are a series of niches along the walls where dishes, containing food as offerings to the gods or the deceased, were placed. The roof of this tomb is flat although some funerary chambers are vaulted. A single extended skeleton was found in the center of the floor of the chamber with additional ce-

Duplicate stone relief of a prisoner impersonating a jaguar with his hands tied behind his back. Panels of glyphs are on the right side of the relief. South Platform, Monte Albán I.

System M is typical of the Classic Monte Albán III structures. To the right is the Danzante *courtyard.*

Architectural detail showing the use of the "open" tablero on the façade of System M, Monte Albán III.

Patio and underground entrance to Tomb 104, Monte Albán III.

ramic bowls that may have contained liquid or food. One of the large, gray-colored funerary urns and four very small urns were in front of the dead person, possibly acting as a guardian for the dead. These objects now can be seen in the Museum of Anthropology in Mexico City where an exact replica has been constructed.

The most remarkable feature of this well-preserved tomb is the lavish mural that extends around the side and end walls. These frescos depict gods, glyphs, and other symbolic objects in a style that is highly formalized and reminiscent of murals in the palace structures at Teotihuacán. The most dramatic deity, painted red and decorated with a bow on his head with additional conventional forms, is placed in the center of the back wall. To his upper right is the glyph 9 Turquoise. On the left side wall is a man in an elaborate headdress wearing beads and earplugs, carrying a baglike object. In front of him is a yellow parrot on a box with a circular

210

object in his mouth. This is followed by a conventionalized serpent with an extended nose-piece surrounded by glyphs. The right wall begins with another figure carrying a bag. In front of him are three elements, one over another, consisting of two glyph elements and a head at the top. The far end of the wall depicts two additional heads, one of a jaguar and the other a bird, each with the glyph 5 under it. The subject of these murals is highly significant, having many religious symbols, but we know little of their meaning today. This tomb with its mural in replica can also be seen at The American Museum of Natural History in New York City.

Just a short distance from Tomb 104 is Tomb 172, a tomb that is well worth a visit as it has been left exactly as it was found. Here are three skeletons lying in the centuries of dust in the chambers with all the bowls, jugs, and other vessels containing offerings which were placed on the floor and niches of the chamber over one thousand years ago.

From here one can proceed along a winding dirt path going directly east for just a short distance and discover Tomb 7, famous because of the quantity of jewels and bone carvings that were found. Tomb 7 was at one time a burial chamber of great architectural beauty for one of the Zapotec dignitaries who lived during the Monte Albán III B Period. Some time after Monte Albán was abandoned by the Zapotecs, the Mixtec Indians moved into the area and utilized some of the Zapotec tombs as burial chambers for their own dead. Tomb 7 is one of these. The tomb was discovered by Alfonso Caso during excavation in 1931–32, and it proved to contain one of the richest treasures of gold ever found in Mesoamerica. This fabulous collection is now housed in the Oaxaca Museum. The Mixtec burial contained the skeletal remains of what might have been a chief or ruler of the time. He was accompanied by several companions. The tomb contained a great horde of silver, gold, turquoise, jade, alabaster, and a great number of bones carved with glyphs as well as other artifacts. Three great funerary urns of the Zapotec Period III were found in the antechamber to the tomb, intentionally broken. They were representations of the Zapotec gods, one of the Old God and two of the Rain God, Cocijo. A replica of this tomb and its superstructure can be seen in the gardens of the Museum of Anthropology in Mexico City.

Scholars who have the time will want to see another of the important tombs here, Tomb 105; however, the tomb chamber is not always open to the public. It is located east of the road leading to Oaxaca on "Plumaje" hill, about half a mile from the Great Plaza. Architecturally it is one of the finest tombs. A portal arch dignifies the entrance to an open court, which is surrounded by chambers. A short stairway leads down to a cruciform-shaped tomb. The murals on the walls are considered by some art historians to be the finest at Monte Albán. Unfortunately, the fresco is badly damaged, and it now can be seen best at the museum in Mexico City where the mural wall to the crypt has been reproduced. Like Tomb 104, the theme of this chamber is religious. There is a series of persons on either side of the tomb, possibly chiefs, dressed in elaborate clothing. Other figures appear in niches and on the other walls, totaling nine male figures and nine female figures. The figure nine may represent the nine Lords of the Night, and the women may well be their consorts. Many glyphs and other iconographic details are spaced between the main elements of the mural.

The paintings in the burial chambers at Monte Albán, as well as those at Cholula, Teotihuacán, and Bonampak, are among our greatest treasures of pre-Conquest times. Other important murals in Mesoamerica have been found at Uaxactún, Chichén Itzá, Tulúm, and Santa Rita de Corozal.

Even though Monte Albán was in constant touch with other great cultures of the time, its physical isolation, midpoint between the Mayas and Teotihuacán, was a major factor in the development of a conservative, distinctive style in architecture and sculpture. Its major contributions include a unique style of architecture, highly formalized tomb murals that are a triumph in fresco painting, and splendid funerary urns that became the major ceramic craft. There is a magical beauty in the mountaintop location of Monte Albán. The architectural structures are well integrated with the landscape, creating a kind of tranquility rare in city planning.

Dainzú

Dainzú is a new name on the map of Mexico. Only recently has excavation begun at this hillside site located near Tlacolula on the road to Mitla. Dainzú is especially significant as it is the only site to date that has incised figures similar to the *Danzante* figures at Monte Albán. These figures were carved in the Middle Preclassic period, possibly as early as 700 B.C. At both sites these large incised slabs were used in the construction of the lower section of pyramid platforms. Both at Dainzú and Monte Albán the male figure is presented with a single idea carved in the stone. At Monte Albán the *Danzantes* are nude, standing figures with knees bent, giving the body a rhythmical movement. The Dainzú figures are more violent in their action and represent players in the ball game.

Dainzú is an extensive site with many mounds still not excavated. There are several plazas, platforms, courtyards, burial chambers, and a partially restored ball court, which is similar to the one at Monte Albán. Above the main plaza and facing the valley below is the pyramid platform of the ball players known as Structure A. The pyramidal base of the platform has vertical walls that may have been broken by a stairway. A later stairway constructed in Late Classic times (Monte Albán III) makes it impossible to determine the kind of a stairway in use in Monte Albán I times, but it would seem there must have been a stairway on the original platform.

Above this platform is another smaller platform that has a central stairway that at one time must have led to some type of sanctuary. This structure faces west in the valley. The lower platform is approximately eighty feet long, and the total length was covered with large stone slabs, most of which were engraved in low relief. Each ball player carries a ball in his

213

General view of the archaeological zone of Dainzú.

Structure A at Dainzú. Stone reliefs are carved on the base of the platform. Middle Preclassic.

hand, and most players have masks to protect their faces, looking somewhat like the masks worn by the catcher in our baseball game today. The ball is much smaller than those noted in ball-game scenes on narrative ceramics, figurines, and bas-reliefs during either the Middle Preclassic or Classic period. We can only assume the game was played quite differently here than in other sections of Mesoamerica.

Around the necks of the ball players at Dainzú is a knotted cord that probably holds on this helmet-type hat. Both arm bands and leg shields are worn to protect the limbs of some players. Accompanying the figures at both sites are hieroglyphs similar to those seen on the *Danzante* figures. These may refer to calendrics, mathematics, or a historical documentation. A large number of the glyphs have not been deciphered, leaving us little information concerning the people of this time. Ignacio Bernal believes there may have been fifty carved stones here originally, but some were missing on excavation and others have lost their image over the years as the sandstone is very friable. Twenty-nine of these figures represent ball players and four depict deities. The very steep hill above this pyramid, called Cerro Dainzú, has five additional figures carved in the same style. These sculptures can be seen by taking a bosky trail up the steep hillside, an eight-hundred-foot climb to the top. The carvings are on natural boulders on an extremely precipitous cliff. En route to the top is evidence of several terraces and a stairway to make access a little easier. This side trip is difficult and should only be undertaken with a competent guide.

Other stones carved in the Dainzú style are found in the villages of Macuilxochitl and Tlacochahuaya, where they are utilized for walls, house foundations, and construction stones for churches and other buildings. Some of these stones are of a later time and in a different style from the above-mentioned Monte Albán I carvings.

The style of the Dainzú ball players and other figures on Structure A are so similar they could well have been done by a single sculptor and his apprentices. Sculptures that are not ball players are the seated jaguar god and human gods carved in curving lines in low relief similar to the other sculptures.

The only other large site in the Americas that has similar incised sculptures on large stone slabs of irregular shape is Cerro Sechín in Peru. Again the subject follows one theme, warriors, and the stones are placed on a similar-shaped wall to that at Dainzú—a high, vertical platform. At Cerro Sechín the carved stones encircle the whole platform, whereas at Dainzú they are only on the façade of the structure. There is no question that the Valley of Oaxaca will yield many more of these early stone carvings in the years to come.

Recent excavations at Dainzú reveal numerous superimpositions of platforms and other structures. On much of the masonry the kind of cement and plaster can be seen. These building materials are some of the earliest used in Mesoamerica. Many tombs have been excavated. One tomb has a great head of a jaguar for the lintel, and the two front legs of the jaguar are incised on stone supports for the lintel on each side of the entrance. This early tomb has a flat roof and is completely constructed with masonry. A small ball player plaque is noted in another tomb nearby, indicating that it dates back to the Middle Preclassic period. Still another tomb is located on the top platform of Structure A. This tomb has a vaulted roof constructed similar to tombs of Monte Albán III period at Monte Albán and probably is from the same period. These tombs have yielded a quantity of pottery. The style of the ceramic objects in the tombs indicates use from Middle Preclassic to Postclassic times. At one stage of the construction (probably Monte Albán III) a very large reservoir, approximately twelve feet square and fourteen feet deep, was built on the hillside. Tapered pipes of baked clay (with a diameter of three and one-half to four inches) are sleeved into each other to carry the water from this reservoir to other parts of the city.

Slightly to the north of this complex of structures in front

Stone relief of a ball player, Structure A, Dainzú. A protective mask is on his head. Middle Preclassic.

of the great platform, Structure A, is a partially reconstructed ball court. This ball court is probably of Monte Albán III B period as it is similar in shape and size to the one at Monte Albán. However, it does not have niches in the diagonal corners of the court, and the stairways are located adjacent to the playing benches. Superstructures were located on the side and end walls of the court and approached by a small stairway on the ends of the buildings. There is evidence that a central shaft (possibly a marker) was inserted into one of the side benches of the court, but the shaft is now missing. A similar shaft hole is noted in the small ball court in front of Tomb 105

217

*Stone relief of deity wearing a jaguar's mask and holding a staff,
Dainzú. Middle Preclassic.*

Partial reconstruction of the ball court, Dainzú. Classic period.

at Monte Albán that is of the Classic period. The Dainzú ball court is slightly larger than the one at Monte Albán.

At Dainzú one can see many transitional phases of architectural style not noted at other sites. Such key structures at Dainzú are great aids for the archaeologist in piecing together the history of a civilization.

Mitla

From colonial times the town of Mitla has used, abused, and encroached upon the finest of Mixtec architecture in Mesoamerica. Fortunately for us, there are still enough structures to sustain Mitla as a popular attraction for visitors. The thirty-mile drive from Oaxaca affords the traveler a chance to see the difference between this valley area and the region farther north. Here the country is more arid, revealing a landscape of faded beige hills occasionally concealed with candelabra cactus and low shrubs that can withstand the long spans of rainless months. However, the rainy season changes this valley into a lush green agricultural bowl that supports the economy of the region. Villages have changed little since the Spanish Conquest. The weekly market affords the townspeople an opportunity to sell their family produce as well as to exchange bits of news and gossip.

The approach to Mitla is on a slight incline where five major groups of ancient buildings are located. Above the city are the remains of old Mixtec forts, and far into the country are burial chambers and many other structures, indicating a heavy population in this valley at one time. When the Spaniards arrived in the sixteenth century, they brought with them diseases unknown to the New World. During the years 1519 to 1600 the population of central Mexico fell from twenty million to one million people, a staggering devastation to the land and ruinous for the Indians.

The valley in which Mitla lies has been occupied by man from very early times. Our first indication of his presence

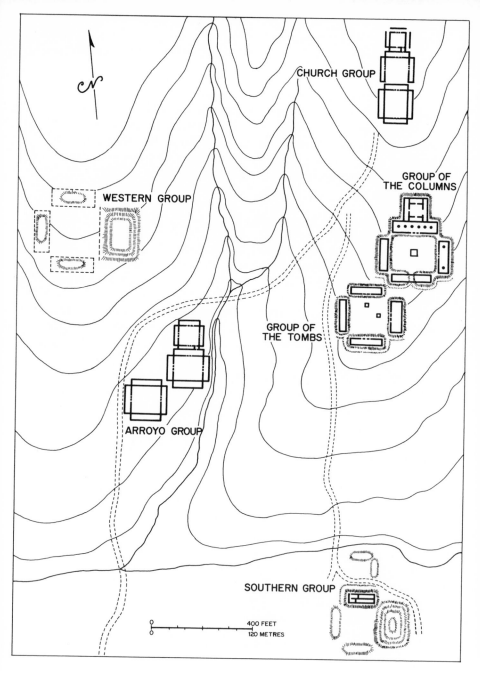

CHURCH GROUP

GROUP OF
THE COLUMNS

WESTERN GROUP

GROUP OF
THE TOMBS

ARROYO GROUP

SOUTHERN GROUP

400 FEET
120 METRES

Mitla (After Holmes)

here is in the Middle Preclassic period (1200–400 B.C.), when he left pottery in burial chambers. Visually there is nothing one can see of this period at Mitla today. The Zapotecs used this area for many centuries during the Classic period, and it has been referred to as the burial grounds of the Zapotec kings. However, we know that most of the great burial chambers of the Zapotecs were located at Monte Albán. One of the five groups of structures at Mitla, the South Group, does show evidence of Zapotec occupation during Monte Albán III B and Monte Albán IV periods (the very end of the classic period and into the early Postclassic period). The Adobe Group is also of an earlier Zapotec period than the existing ruins at Mitla. Both of these groups are in very poor condition and appear only as mounds today.

The two groups best known at Mitla are the Church Group and the Palace Group, where the Hall of Columns and the Patio of the Tombs are located. According to John Paddock, these structures were built during Monte Albán V period just prior to the Spanish Conquest. The similarities of the structures at Mitla and Yagul are striking. Most of the Mixtec structures are palace or civic groups rather than the religious structures predominant at Monte Albán. The Mixtecs had a long history, influencing areas from the Oaxaca Valley to as far north as the Toluca Valley. By the eighth century A.D. they were developing their own art styles in many of the fine craft techniques, and they continued to excel in this field until the sixteenth century. Their exquisite goldwork, fine cut stones in rock crystal and obsidian, craftsmanship in manuscript writing and illustration, and expertness in the making of mosaic masks and other objects has not been equaled. Many of these precious objects have been found in burials at the Mixtec sites of Zaachila, Yagul, and Mitla. It was at Mitla, however, that they achieved their greatest mastery in architecture. The Group of the Columns is the most distinguished structure of all the palaces the Mixtecs ever built.

221

Exterior façade of the Hall of Columns, Palace Group, Mitla. Post-classic.

The Mixtecs employed the *tablero* and *talud* for their buildings, but they used these devices quite differently from the Zapotecs at Monte Albán. The *tablero* was decorated in mosaic of extremely fine cut stones worked on both the exterior and interior of their buildings into a variety of fret designs. The *talud* on the exterior walls of the palace was reserved for the base of the structure abutting the platform. The Mixtec architects employed eight stepped fret designs throughout this large palace. Several of these designs were often incorporated in one room, creating extremely "busy" walls. Technically the stone is superbly cut, fitting together precisely without the use of mortar. It is reported that there are over 100,000 cut

222

Entrance to the Hall of Columns, Palace Group, Mitla. Stone lintels over the doorway are monolithic. Postclassic.

stones in the Building of the Columns. The masonry construction at Mitla is one in which the core of the walls is of cut stone and clay. This is then faced with the fine cut mosaic stones. The technique of "false mosaic" was also employed in which a monolithic stone was carved in a fret design to look like the other mosaic patterns. Lintels over doorways as well as other structural stones were cut in this fashion. The fret pattern became an obsession with the architects of the time.

The Group of the Columns is composed of three masonry halls resting on raised platforms that open into a very large, square-shaped, sunken courtyard. The north hall, The Hall of Columns, is enlarged to include a series of chambers, be-

223

Six monolithic columns at one time supported the roof of the Hall of Columns, Palace Group, Mitla. Postclassic.

Interior detail in the Hall of Columns showing the mosaic stones used within the tablero. Postclassic.

Mosaic stone decoration used for the interior of the Palace rooms, Mitla. No mortar was used.

coming a palace-type structure. A triple doorway, with mammoth monolithic lintels, opens into an unusually long room measuring 132 feet in length with a width of 24 feet. Six monolithic conical columns, over twelve feet high, at one time supported a roof for this hall. Today the roof is open to the sky.

To the north of the great Hall of Columns is a narrow passageway, with an extremely low roof, that leads to a patio. On all sides are chambers decorated with mosaic stone. One of the chambers has had the roof reconstructed of bamboo and wooden beams in order to protect the mosaics from further deterioration. The three other rooms are also in mosaic stone but not as well preserved.

In front of the Hall of Columns is a very large courtyard which was surrounded by other structures similar to the Hall of Columns. However, today little of the ruins remain to be seen. In the center of this courtyard is a raised platform that may have been used as an *adoratorio* in ancient times. These many buildings and the courtyard still have plaster and some red paint remaining on the exterior surfaces.

Adjacent to the Hall of Columns is the Palace of the Tombs, quite similar in plan to the complex that includes the Hall of Columns. On one of the sides of this large courtyard are the remains of porticoed chambers. The portico had three entrances. All have circular holes at the sides of the doorways which were used for wooden beams projecting into the platform. These surely must have supported canopies of cotton cloth that would shade the elite while they enjoyed the ceremonies in the courtyard below. The lintels of stone are the largest at Mitla and weigh approximately twenty-five tons each.

On the east side of the courtyard to the Palace of the Tombs is a stairway leading along an extremely low entranceway to a cruciform chamber under the patio floor. This chamber is also decorated with beautifully cut "false mosaic" frets on monolithic slabs of stone. The chamber was a very large burial area, but looters cleaned it out centuries ago and the contents are unknown. For the convenience of the visitor, the chamber now has electric lights. Another burial chamber is on the north side of the courtyard, and this one is decorated in true mosaic stones. Plaster on the walls of the tomb and the courtyard floor still retains the original red paint. These burial chambers at Mitla are good-sized rooms that make it possible for the visitor to walk around inside of them. The ceiling stones of the chambers are the floor stones of the courtyard, indicating the complex was planned as a burial area as well as a ceremonial center.

The walk is short from the Building of the Columns to the Church Group. This group is also a palace-type structure similar to the one just described, but smaller. However, a Spanish church was placed where part of this palace existed, and the palace stones were used to build it. Nevertheless,

226

The Church Group at Mitla was another palace-type structure similar to the Palace Group. In colonial times a Spanish church was built in one of the large courtyards, and much of the ancient palace was destroyed. Postclassic.

there is still a section of the palace that is interesting for the traveler to visit. Still surviving are two patios enclosed by walls that are in the same style as the Hall of the Columns. In the smaller patio can be seen the last traces of mural painting, most of it having disintegrated by weathering. Enough of the painting is still visible to note that the style is Mixtec, and it resembles very closely that seen in Mixtec codices. This style of painting was also used at Tulúm and Santa Rita de Corozal in the southern area of Mesoamerica. A series of chambers decorated in stone mosaic opens into this small patio at Mitla. Originally the projecting mosaic stones were painted white against a background of deep red. This contrasted sharply with the more delicate mural in red and white. The rest of the walls, as well as the patio floors, were in deep red, giving a completely different visual impression to that of the natural stone as we see it today.

The use of mosaic stones for decorating the exterior of buildings is not an original idea with the Mixtecs. In Oaxaca it was used as early as Monte Albán II period (400 B.C.–A.D. 1). We also see it used at Teotihuacán in the Palace of Quetzal-papalotl. Shortly after this time the Mayas were using mosaic stones for their structures at Uxmal, Kabah, Labná, and other sites in the Puuc Hills as well as other areas in Yucatán. At the Classic site of El Tajín in Veracruz, mosaic stonework was also important in the architecture. However, the Mixtecs at Mitla were remarkable in their refinement of a single idea in architecture—that is, the handling of large, undecorated mono-lithic structural stones in conjunction with the delicacy of fine cut mosaic decorative panels.

There are three other groups of structures at Mitla that have not been reconstructed. Two of these are adobe, and today they look like mud mounds. A church has been built on top of the Adobe Group, but it is no longer used. Stones from the Arroyo Group have been used for village construction. It is unfortunate that these most expressive architectural forms used by the Mixtecs met with such devastating destruction by the Spaniards.

Lambityeco

Close to the time the Zapotecs were to abandon their city of Monte Albán, Lambityeco was becoming important among the Zapotec rulers, continuing a culture that for unknown circumstances was to climax at their capital. The archaeological city of Lambityeco is extremely important as it was completely constructed in Monte Albán III and IV, little known by archaeologists outside of Monte Albán. Now this segment of Zapotec history can be more fully analyzed.

Lambityeco is approximately three miles north of Yagul on the main highway to Oaxaca. It consists of a large group of mounds that are all believed to be Terminal Classic (A.D. 700–900). This time period in Mesoamerican history reflects a shifting of power from the great classical sites of Teotihuacán, Cholula, and Monte Albán to new ascending tribal groups with powerful chieftains such as the Mixtecs and Toltecs. These new political alignments were felt in the Toluca Valley, the Valley of Morelos, and the Valley of Mexico. The Mixtecs had already established themselves in the Cholula-Puebla area and were now looking south for new areas to set up ruling families. Their presence was felt in the first three centuries of the Postclassic period (A.D. 900–1200), but it was during the last two centuries before the Spanish Conquest that the large palaces at Mitla were built and Yagul came into prominence.

During the early part of this turbulent period the Zapotecs were shifting their seat of control from Monte Albán to a more southerly location. Early structures at Mitla are Zapotec as are several other ancient sites in the area. The Lambityeco site consists of two or three dozen mounds scattered over a large area of the countryside. Because of leveling over the farm area, it is hard to determine whether all the present mounds are ancient. It is quite possible that some of the ruins are located under the nearby village of Tlacolula. Lambityeco came under the influence of the Mixtecs at a very early time. It was here that the Mixtecs were to develop the style of the step-fret popularly used at Mitla in Period V. Lambityeco was abandoned at the end of Period IV, and the Mixtecs are believed to have shifted their control of the valley to Yagul.

From the roadside, the first structure at Lambityeco to be noted is a small pyramid complex partially restored by archaeologists. It faces a small patio which has a platform in the center, possibly used as an *adoratorio.* In the construction, the masons used broken pottery sherds, set horizontally in layers, as a part of the vertical walls, which were then plastered over and painted.

While excavating the pyramid, archaeologists discovered an earlier superimposition, possibly a dwelling, and restored

Frieze of four heads carved in stucco in the tomb area of Lambityeco. Postclassic.

the façade. On the top part of the façade were four carved stucco panels. Two of these remain today. Below these panels and at the base of the structure is Tomb 5. Above the doorway to the tomb is a carved stucco decorative panel of two heads, believed to be a man (a moustache is noted on one) and a woman. These persons may have been the residents of the dwelling. Their names are recorded as 1 Movement and 10 Reed. Later in the history of this complex, the dwelling and tomb were covered over by a small pyramid. A temple-type structure was constructed on top of the pyramid, but only the foundations of the rooms remain today.

Adjacent to this pyramid is a similar structure with several reconstructions. Under these reconstructions is Tomb 2, with two large sculptured heads of the Zapotec god, Cocijo. Here we see the slightly decadent style of Monte Albán IV. On the vertical walls of the courtyard to the tomb can be seen a decorative stepped-fret design. This design was next to be used in a very elaborate way on the walls of structures at Yagul. This style of mosaic decoration reached its florescence at the Mixtec site of Mitla.

One of the two large heads of the God of Fertility, Cocijo, at Lambit-yeco. This tomb decoration is in a decadent style and possibly dates just prior to the Spanish conquest.

Lambityeco was abandoned at the end of Period IV, and shortly after this time the Mixtecs were constructing another strategic city, Yagul.

Yagul

The hilltop site of Yagul, crowned by a fortress, rises out of the mild, misty valley like a ghost ship appearing at sea. It seems natural that migrating people would choose the hillside for settlement in their early history. The surrounding valley was fertile; the hill location would prominently display their city to good advantage; the promontory at the hilltop was an ideal lookout station for any military disturbance in the valley below; and the land elevation would pick up any cool breeze to temper the tantalizing hot afternoon sun.

Yagul is approximately eight miles from Mitla on the main highway to Oaxaca. A paved road, going north half a mile, leads to the site. Man has occupied this hilltop from the beginning of the occupation of the valley. During excavation, four tombs were discovered with burials from the Monte Albán I period (800–400 B.C.). These tombs were structurally the same as those of the same period at Monte Albán except that at Yagul they were constructed of adobe rather than stone. In Mesoamerica burial chambers of adobe are extremely rare. In these chambers were found ceramic pieces that are related to those at Monte Albán. During Late Classic times (Monte Albán III B and IV) Yagul was occupied by the Zapotecs. When the Mixtecs came into the area in Late Postclassic times, they destroyed or built over the earlier structures, and what we see today is all Mixtec and is referred to as Period V.

The climb along a dirt path to reach the Great Fortress on the hilltop is not difficult, and the view from the top gives quite a handsome panorama of the surrounding countryside. The scattered ruins of an extensive fortified wall as well as platforms, plazas, and tombs are located atop this hillside,

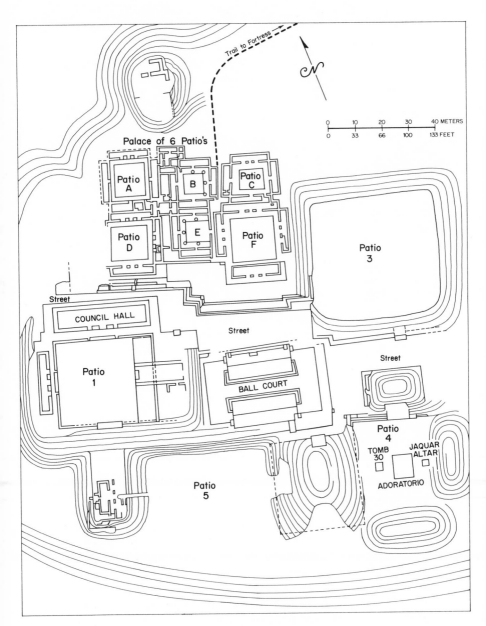

Yagul (After Leobardo de la Luz Merino)

233

General view of the Mixtec ruins at Yagul. To the left can be seen the ball court, the Palace of the Six Patios on the right.

all built by the Mixtecs. One of the tombs in pure Mixtec style, Tomb 28, can be entered by descending a stairway at the top of the path on the east side of the hill. These steps lead down to an underground chamber constructed of cut stone. A monolithic slab of stone covered the entrance door to the tomb chamber. The stone lintel over the tomb door is carved in relief with two jaguar heads on either end and an unknown glyph in the central portion. Inside this door is a second chamber with another carved lintel. The second lintel has a parrot carved in low relief on the left side, a central glyph, and a jaguar head on the right side of the lintel. Glyphs are Mixtec and indicate a Postclassic burial. The tomb was looted many centuries ago. Mixtec polychrome pottery has been found in all the tombs of Monte Albán V period. The tombs at Yagul,

234

Carved panel of glyphs decorates the stone used to block the entrance of Tomb 28, Yagul. Postclassic.

in triple grouping, are the only ones at right angles to each other in Mexico except for the Valley of Toluca site, Calixtla-huaca. Most of the tomb façades are decorated in a step-fret mosaic design not used by the Zapotecs at Monte Albán. Yagul tombs are not as large or as grand in appearance as those at Monte Albán; however, the architectural style of the tombs is basically the same.

To the east of the Great Fortress is a tremendously large stone pinnacle that was utilized by the Mixtecs as a lookout tower. It was reached by a narrow walk over a natural land saddle. The saddle was filled in with a five-foot wall of stone which acts as a bridge to the tower. From here the ancient ruins of the city below are dramatically silhouetted by the afternoon sun.

Section of the Palace of Six Patios, Yagul, showing the maze of rooms. Postclassic.

Flanking the hillside and reaching out into the plains were the dwellings of the Mixtec people. The area reserved for the chieftains, priests, and elite members of society, known as the Acropolis, abuts the hill. This consists of several patios surrounded by structures, a great area known as the Palace of the Six Patios, and a ball court, recently restored. Of course numerous other structures are buried here under the many mounds awaiting the spade of future archaeologists. At the present time thirty tombs have been uncovered in this area, giving us an insight into the Mixtec religious ceremonial activities. Materials in these tombs are important to archaeologists as some of it can be used for carbon dating. Data such as this, as well as other factors, help toward the accuracy of a chronological sequence for occupation.

A street, moving in angles from east to west, separates the north and south sections of the archaeological zone at

236

Patio F, Palace of Six Patios, Yagul. This courtyard is the largest in the palace.

Yagul. The wall on the north and south sides of this street were decorated with stone mosaics, and some of these cut stones still can be seen today. To the north of this street is the Palace of the Six Patios, now a labyrinth of walls creating a maze that would make any intrepid traveler confused if not downright muddled. The Palace is formal in arrangement, divided into six patios that are surrounded by a variety of chambers. Each of these sections is constructed differently, and the size of the patios and chambers vary greatly. The walls of the rooms were first made of clay and stone. Next, they were faced with dressed stone, plastered, and painted red. Much of the original plaster and paint can be seen today.

Patio F is quite obviously the most important section of the palace and no doubt was reserved for the ruling chief, with the adjoining rooms for his wives and other members of the family. In excavating here, five superimpositions were found

237

below the palace floor, and at a depth of twenty feet yielding the good stratigraphic cross section so important in dating structures. The earliest floor proved to be Zapotec of the Monte Albán III B and IV periods. Patio F has three adjoining rooms with easy access to Patio C to the north. The rooms on the west side of the palace contained tombs, but there is no evidence of them today. The arrangement of rooms in the Palace is very similar to those in the Church Group at Mitla, especially Patios F and C. The general style of the Palace rooms opening on a sunken courtyard had been used since Early Classic times at Teotihuacán. This patio-style architecture next appeared at Xochicalco, and then at Tula. It was also popular with the Mixtec and Aztec elite.

In the southwest sector of the Yagul archaeological zone is a large ceremonial courtyard designated as Patio 1. Although only partially restored, this impressive area must have been very important in its time. It is another area where many tombs have been found. A great hall, referred to as the Council Chamber, runs the length of the patio to the north, and at one time was decorated with stone mosaics, but none remain today. The chamber seems aptly named as it is over seventy feet long, but it may never be known just what purpose this unusually long room may have served.

From Patio 1 is a splendid view of the newly restored ball court. Ball courts throughout Mesoamerica are quite uniform in shape over a period of one thousand years. Variations did exist in size, placement of stairs, use of markers and rings, and the nature of the associated chambers. This particular ball court is the largest in the Oaxaca Valley, measuring approximately 125 feet in length. In shape it is very similar to the ball court at Dainzú and the one at Monte Albán, built some centuries earlier by the Zapotecs. Although most Postclassic ball courts have rings on the vertical side walls such as those seen at Xochicalco, Tula, and Chichén Itzá, rings were not used on this court. However, a stone marker in the shape of a serpent's head was found in the south wall of the court and most likely was used as a method of scoring. Serpent

The ball court at Yagul, built by the Mixtecs, has been completely restored and is very similar to the court at Monte Albán built by the Zapotecs. Postclassic.

heads, placed in a similar fashion, were used as markers for the ball court at Mixco Viejo in Guatemala. Both courts are similar and fall in the same Late Postclassic period. The Postclassic period in the Guatemala highlands shows influence of the Mexican style at Iximché, Zaculeu, and Mixco Viejo as well as at other Maya sites.

Adjacent to the ball court at Yagul is Patio 4, with an assembly of mounds bordering the four sides. The patio is sometimes referred to as the Patio of the Triple Tomb. There is a low platform in the center of the patio probably used for an *adoratorio*. Just to the west of this shrine is a stairway leading under the courtyard to three tombs, each in the shape of a "T." This group of tombs, possibly built before the patio was constructed, are all stone-faced, and the *tableros* are carved

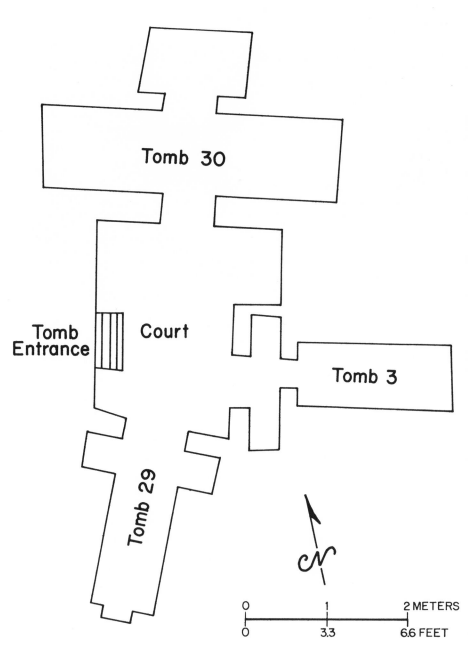

Tomb 30

Tomb
Entrance

Court

Tomb 3

Tomb 29

N

| 0 | | 1 | | 2 METERS |
| 0 | | 3.3 | | 6.6 FEET |

Triple Tomb Complex in Patio 4, Yagul

*Entrance to Tomb 30 located in the Patio of the Triple Tomb, Yagul.
Postclassic.*

in the Mixtec step-fret design. Tomb 30, the largest of the three
tombs, has two tenoned heads placed on either side of the
entrance. The monolithic stone covering the door to Tomb 30
has an over-all greco design carved in low relief on both sides.
In excavating the tomb, Paddock found that it had been looted
at a very early time. However, the looters did not discover the
tomb recesses. Here were found a large number of bodies,
possibly from burials over a long period. Later burials neces-
sitated the pushing back of previous burials toward the wall —
thus the disarray of the tomb contents. This has been noted
in other burials both at Zapotec and Mixtec sites.

In front of Mound 4E, to the east, is a very large stone
carving of a roughly shaped and badly eroded animal form.
It could have been a jaguar, but today, with weathering, it
looks very much like a gigantic toad with a depression on

Jaguar-like animal located near Mound 4E, Yagul. A depression in the animal's back could have been used for an offering. Postclassic.

his back for offerings. The Mixtecs were not carvers of large sculptures, and the style of this particular animal has a simplcity that is more closely related to Olmec or Olmecoid sculpture. Its presence here leaves unanswered, possibly for all time, who the artists were who may have created this toadlike sculpture, the culture they expressed, and the ceremonial use or meaning of this unusually large animal form.

For many years Mitla was the only Mixtec city for the traveler to visit. Now there is Yagul, which is at least in part contemporary with Mitla. Yagul does not have the grandeur of Mitla nor is it as well preserved, but there is a natural beauty at Yagul where the Mixtec architects have harmoniously integrated their close-knit city plan to this hilltop terrain.

Zaachila

Just ten miles south of Oaxaca is the little village of Villa de Zaachila. The town has no great distinction, but market day brings a flurry of activity and it is a pleasant day to make a visit. According to the codices, after the Zapotec kings abandoned Monte Albán, Zaachila became their capital. According to other sources, Mitla was the important city of the Zapotecs after Monte Albán came to an end. However, at some time prior to the Spanish Conquest the area was taken over by the Mixtecs. During this time the valley was a rich one, and the Mixtec ruling class, swathed in the wealth of luxury trade items, could well afford to adorn themselves with elegant gold jewelry made by their superlative craftsmen and to have these placed, along with other heirloom treasures, in their elaborate tombs.

In the town of Zaachila are many indications of ancient occupation. Mounds are seen in the center of the village and near the church. The townspeople have been reluctant to permit excavation. Because of violent villager outbursts, Alfonso Caso was forced to flee in 1942. Ignacio Bernal met the same experience in 1953.

In 1962 the most important find at Zaachila was two tombs in Mound A next to the Castillo mound in the center of the village. These were excavated by Roberto Gallegos under armed guard. The tombs are located beneath a large Mixtec patio with the foundation of rooms as a part of the same complex. The façades of these two tombs are in typical Mixtec style, decorated with mosaic stone. From the style of the polychrome pottery, bone carving, gold pieces, and turquoise mosaics, both of these tombs are of Monte Albán V period and are probably contemporary with the Mixtec contents of Tomb 7 at Monte Albán. In 1971 two additional tombs were dis-

The exposed foundation of the patio to Tomb 1, Zaachila. The sunken court was enclosed by superstructures. The tomb is reached by a stairway under the courtyard. Postclassic period. Courtesy Elaine Burleigh.

Stucco sculpture of an owl on the wall of the antechamber to the Zaachila tomb. The owl may represent a guardian deity. Postclassic period. Courtesy Shirley Thompson.

Relief sculpture on the interior chamber of the Zaachila tomb. This figure may represent one of the Lords of the Night. Postclassic period. Courtesy Shirley Thompson.

245

Relief sculpture representing 9 Flower on the interior wall of Tomb 1, Zaachila. There are seven major sculptures in relief in this tomb. Postclassic period. Courtesy Shirley Thompson.

246

covered in the San Sebastián neighborhood of Zaachila.

As one enters Tomb 1 at Zaachila, there are two stone jaguar heads tenoned into the façade. Next is an antechamber. The two vertical side walls have sculptured stucco plaques of two large owls with outspread wings. They may be protectors of the tomb, hovering over the area as deities of darkness. Below these owl wall plaques are two niches. The main burial chamber is also decorated with two stucco deities, possibly Lords of the Night. They are accompanied by two additional male figures dressed in ceremonial clothing and holding what seem to be large handbags, possibly for incense. Glyphically these two figures are designated 9 Flower and 5 Flower. On the wall at the rear of the tomb is another plaster sculpture of a deity placed horizontally on the wall. His head emerges from a serpent's jaw and his body is covered by a tortoise shell. This sculpture as well as the others in the tomb are painted flesh-pink.

In the niches and scattered on the floor were many types of ceramics including polychrome pottery from Period V, bone remains of the buried, and adornments worn by these rich Mixtec rulers.

Tomb 2 is not as elaborate, but the great treasure within it produced a superb collection of gold, bone carving, and jade. One of the great pieces from this tomb is a disc of glittering gold with mosaic stones set in a medallion in the center of the disc. This handsome work of craftsmanship can be seen in the Museum of Anthropology in Mexico City. The other precious pieces from this tomb are also on display at this museum. Especially fine are the deer, jaguar, and human bones incised with glyphs referring to rituals, the calendar, and historical events. There is a great variety of polychrome pottery, one small cup from Tomb 1 having a blue hummingbird on its rim. The gold jewelry is quite similar to that of Tomb 7 at Monte Albán, but here there were not as many pieces. Another of the important artifacts found in Tomb 2 is a carved jade handle, possibly for a fan, in which an exquisite head

247

of a serpent is fashioned. These tomb treasures give us some idea of the significance of luxury goods and the religious cere- monies that must have been part of burials for the great men of the time.

Suggestions for Reaching
Archaeological Zones

All of the archaeological zones in Mexico can be reached by car. At Malinalco a standard car will not be sufficient because of the difficult road, and therefore it is necessary to switch at the village of Tenancingo to a taxi or bus built especially for these roads. Local buses go to some of the villages where archaeological zones are located, but it is advisable to take them only if you know some Spanish. There are very few planned or packaged tours that go to the ancient ruins. Of course, it is easy enough to see Teotihuacán, for daily guided trips are offered by several travel agencies in Mexico City. At Oaxaca the scheduled tours only go to Mitla and Monte Albán.

It is advisable to hire a car if you wish to see more than three or four of the major ruins. Finding a scholarly guide to interpret the sites is more difficult.

Cuicuilco and Copilco: These ruins are located near the University of Mexico on the highway to Cuernavaca. By car your drive will be along Avenida Insurgentes, continuing a short distance past the university until you see a sign for the Cuicuilco site. It is a very large but low-lying mound on the left-hand side of the highway. Copilco is nearby. Since Copilco is not always open, you should inquire about it while at the little museum in Cuicuilco.

Both *Tenayuca* and *Santa Cecilia* can be reached by car by following the Laredo highway to Calzada de Vallejo and on to Tenayuca, approximately six miles from downtown Mexico City. Santa Cecilia is only about one mile from Tenayuca.

Tula is approximately sixty-five miles north of Mexico

249

City on the highway to Laredo. An interesting visit en route is at Tepotzotlan. This old, historical town has a very beautiful cathedral and religious museum. Adjacent to it is a monastery where a delightful lunch is served.

Calixtlahuaca can be reached by car, bus, or train. For train travel, take the line to Morelia and get off at Toluca. From here a taxi will be needed. By bus or car, you proceed to Toluca. From there the drive to Calixtlahuaca is approximately ten miles. It is necessary to take the highway in the direction of Ixtlahuaca to arrive at the ruins near the town of Cuidad Juárez.

Malinalco can be reached by car by taking the highway to Toluca. Before reaching Toluca you will encounter an intersection located at La Marquesa where you must turn left. This is a new road, which has been completed to Chalma. From Chalma you can continue the drive to Malinalco. From the village of Malinalco there is a footpath that leads to the top of a very steep slope where the ancient ruins are located. This walk takes about half an hour.

Teopanzolco is in Cuernavaca and can be seen by going just "over the railroad tracks." You can see the ruins from there.

Xochicalco can only be reached by car. It is approximately twenty-eight miles from Cuernavaca. Leave Cuernavaca on the highway to Acapulco, then at Alpuyeca proceed on the road to the Caves of Cacahuamilpa until the sign for Xochicalco appears. There is a two-mile drive up the mountainside to the ruins after leaving the main road.

Teotihuacán is just twenty-five miles north of Mexico City on the highway to Laredo, easily reached by car. Many of the tour agencies have daily bus tours to this archaeological zone. These groups do not go into Tetitla, Atetelco, or Tepantitla to see the murals, but only tour the central ceremonial center.

Cholula is on the highway to Puebla, approximately two hours from Mexico City and just eight miles from Puebla.

Zempoala is approximately 275 miles from Mexico City. There is plane and bus service to Veracruz. From here it is necessary to use a car to reach the ruins. Leaving Veracruz, proceed on the road to Jalapa until you reach the village of El Tamaraindo, and at this point take the coastal highway north to Zempoala.

El Tajín is approximately 220 miles from Mexico City and can be reached by car or plane to Poza Rica. From here it is only eight miles to the ruins of El Tajín.

Monte Albán is only six miles outside of Oaxaca and can be reached by car as the road is completely paved. There are daily flights from Mexico City to Oaxaca.

Zaachila is south of Oaxaca on the road to Xoxocatlan. Continuing beyond Cuilapan is Villa de Zaachila, approximately nine miles from Oaxaca.

Mitla, Lambityeco, Dainzú, and *Yagul* are all on the international highway en route to the Isthmus of Tehuantepec. Mitla, the most distant of these four ancient ruins is approximately twenty-five miles from Oaxaca.

Since most of the ancient ruins are in remote areas, it is advisable to take a box lunch so that you do have a full day for exploration. Usually there is a soft drink stand somewhere nearby for refreshments.

There are five museums that are important for archaeological collections, the most famous being the Museo Nacional de Antropologia e Historia in Mexico City. Also in Mexico City is the Anahuacalli Museo that houses the collection given to the country by Diego Rivera. The Cortés Palace is now restored in Cuernavaca and has a fine collection of colonial and archaeological pieces. In Oaxaca is the Museo Regional de Oaxaca, recently opened in the monastery of Santo Domingo, and here is located the treasure from Tomb 7 at Monte Albán. However, the museum is much more extensive, with an ethnographical collection as well as colonial art. Also in Oaxaca is the new museum that houses the Tamayo archaeological collection, and is known as the Rufino Tamayo Museum of Mexico's Prehispanic Art.

Selected Readings

Bernal, Ignacio. *The Olmec World*. Berkeley, 1969.
———. *Mexico: Pre-Hispanic Paintings*. Greenwich, 1958.
Brundage, Burr Cartwright. *A Rain of Darts*. Austin, 1972.
Bushnell, G. H. S. *Ancient Arts of the Americas*. New York, 1965.
Caso, Alfonso. *The Aztecs: People of the Sun*. Norman, 1958.
Coe, Michael D. *America's First Civilization*. New York, 1968.
———. *Mexico*. New York, 1962.
Covarrubias, Miguel. *The Indian Art of Mexico and Central America*. New York, 1957.
Díaz del Castillo, Bernal. *Discovery and Conquest of Mexico*. New York, 1956.
Hunter, C. Bruce. *A Guide to Ancient Maya Ruins*. Norman, 1974.
Kubler, George. *The Art and Architecture of Ancient America*. Harmondsworth, 1962.
Lothrop, Samuel K., and others. *Essays in Pre-Columbian Art and Archaeology*. Cambridge, 1964.
Marquina, Ignacio. *Arquitectura Prehispanica*. Mexico, 1951.
Paddock, John. *Ancient Oaxaca*. Stanford, 1966.
Pollock, H. E. D. *Round Structures of Aboriginal Middle America*. Washington, 1936.
Porter, Muriel N. *Tlatilco and the Pre-Classic Cultures of the New World*. New York, 1953.
Sanders, William T., and Barbara J. Price. *Mesoamerica: The Evolution of a Civilization*. New York, 1968.
Soustelle, Jacques. *Daily Life of the Aztecs*. Stanford, 1970.
Vaillant, George C. *Aztecs of Mexico*. Harmondsworth, 1966.
Wauchope, R., editor. *Handbook of Middle American Indians*. Vols. 1–4, 10, 11. Austin, 1964.
Wolf, Eric. *Sons of the Shaking Earth*. Chicago, 1959.

Index

255

A Guide to Ancient Mexican Ruins

82–83, 92–93; ball court, 78, 238; sculpture, 81; paintings, 212
Chichimec tribes: 74, 93, 131
Cholula: 10, 29, 31, 58, 61, 74, 92, 106, 131, 146, 153, 212; pyramid of Cholula, 59, 69; population, 59; focal point of culture, 60; construction materials, 61; ceremonial center, 61–62; Pyramid C, 61–63; Pyramids A and B, 62; Great Plaza (Patio de los Altares), 63–67; monuments, 63, 66–67; murals, 63–66; stairways, 66–67; pottery, 71–73
Cholula-Puebla area: 73, 229
Church of *Nuestra Señora de los Remedios*: 59
Cielito: 92
Classic period: 3, 10, 12, 22–23, 29, 56–57, 70–71, 75, 122, 124, 131, 146, 153, 160, 176, 198–99, 201, 215, 221, 228, 232
Coatepec: 18
Cocijo (rain god): 207, 212, 230
Comisión Cientifica Exploradora: 179
Copán: 135, 141, 143, 153
Copilco: 3–4, 9, 190; political organization, 17
Cortés, Hernando: 12, 113, 150, 176, 181, 184
Cortes Palace, Cuernavaca: 145, 149–50
Cuacuahtinchan (Temple of the Sun): *see* Malinalco (Structure I)
Cuernavaca: 130, 146, 149
Cuicuilco: 9; political organization, 17; architecture, 17–23, 178; ceremonial center, 22–23

Dainzú: 9, 187, 192; sculptures, 195, 213–19; Structure A, 213–17; burial chambers, tombs, 212, 216–18; ball court, 213–19, 238; ball game, 213–16; glyphs, 215; Cerro Dainzú, 215; superstructures, 216–17; reservoir, 216
Deities: 22, 34, 41, 61, 71, 75, 99,

116, 118–19, 138, 173, 190, 198–99, 201, 215
Díaz, Bernal: 178
Drainage systems: 40, 69, 119; at Zempoala, 178
Dwellings: 18, 59, 87–88, 90, 130, 169, 187, 230
Dzibilchaltún: 35, 190

Early Classic period: 153, 200, 238
Early Postclassic period: 12, 122–23, 146, 149
Early Preclassic period: 3, 185
Earth goddess, Coatlicue: 109, 184
El Arbolillo: 3, 18
El Salvador: 6, 10, 73
El Tajín: 29, 33, 61, 92, 136, 143, 228; Veracruz Classic capital, 151, 153; ball game ceremonies, 151, 160–67, 173; pottery, 151; ceramics, 151; figurines, 151, 173–75; ceremonial center, 151, 159; architecture, 153; Pyramid of the Niches complex, 153–57; El Tajín Chico, 153, 167–73; "flying cornices," 154–60, 172; platforms, 156–60, 172; Structures 2 and 5, 157–59, 165; superimpositions, 157, 159, 169–72; stelae, 159; Structure 15, 159; Structures 3 and 23, 159–60, 169; ball courts, 160–67; Structure K, 169; Structure C, 169; plaza, 169; Structure B, 169; Structure D, 169; Structure A, 171–72, 195; murals, 172; Structure Q, 173; Building of the Columns, 173; Building of the Tunnels, 173; glyphs, 173; abandoned, 176; *see also* figurines

"False mosaic": 223, 226
Figurines, figures: 3–4, 18, 24, 138, 190–92, 195, 201, 215; "laughing faces," 151, 173–75; rain god, Cocijo, 207, 212; *see also* El Tajín
Flying cornices at El Tajín: 154–60, 172

256

219, 221–28; burial chambers, tombs, 219–21, 226; and Zapotecs, 221–22; South Group, 221; Adobe Group, 221, 228; Church Group, 221, 226, 238; Palace Group, 221, 226; Hall of Columns, Group of Columns, 221–28; Patio of the Tombs, Palace of the Tombs, 221, 226; mosaics, 223–28; Arroyo Group, 228

Mixcoatl ("Cloud Serpent"): 75

Mixco Viejo: 239

Mixteca (pottery style): 73

Mixtec-Puebla area: 131

Mixtecs: 12, 74, 102, 131, 137, 179, 229–32, 238, 241–43; pottery, 87; glyphs, 138; at Monte Albán, 189, 211; at Mitla, 219, 221–28

Moctezuma, Don Pedro: 92

Moctezuma, Rodrigo de Paz: 94

Moctezuma II: 123, 129, 181, 184

Monte Albán: 9, 29, 33, 56–57, 89, 92, 131, 141, 229; controlled by Zapotecs, 12, 189, 222, 228, 234, 243; tombs, 40, 104–105, 187, 189, 199, 201, 205, 211–12, 218, 221, 247; agriculture, 185; artisans, 185–87; dwellings, 187; city, ceremonial centers, 187, 199; murals, 189, 198–99, 210–12; Southern Platform, 189, 205; Great Plaza, 189, 193, 198–99, 205, 212; ball court, 189, 195, 201–202, 218; epochs of, 189–90, 192–95, 198–99, 202, 205, 211–12, 215–18, 221, 228, 230, 232, 238, 243; and Mixtecs, 189; glyphs, 190–95, 200, 210–12; *Danzante* building figures, 190–92, 201, 205, 207, 213, 215; Building J (Observatory), 193, 195; superimpositions, 195, 202; stelae, 195–98, 200, 205; funerary chambers, urns, 198–99, 207–10; government, 198; North Platform, 199–201, 207

Monte Negro: 190

Montes de Mixtongo: 113

Monuments: 63, 66–67, 70, 176, 195; Tizoc Stone, 123; at Xochicalco, 139; *see also* stelae

Morend, Jiménez: 75

Mosaics: 223–28

Murals: 22, 28, 61, 147; at Teotihuacán, 36–58, 153; at Cholula, 63–66; at Tula, 92; at Tlatelolco, 110–11; at Tajín, 172; at Monte Albán, 189, 198–99, 210–12

Museo Nacional de Antropologia e Historia, Mexico City, D. F.: 9, 55, 165, 198

Museum of Anthropology, Mexico City, D. F.: 33, 85, 112, 123, 138, 141, 212, 247

Nahuatl language: 74, 94, 131, 137

Nicaragua: 73

Noguera, Eduardo: 137

Nopaltzin: 93

Oaxaca: 9, 212, 219, 228–29, 232, 243

Obsidian: 23, 33, 52, 84, 138

Olmec civilization: 4, 6, 8–9, 18, 198, 242; sculptures, 9–10; cites, 9, 190

Oztotitlan: 195

Paddock, John: 221, 241

Palaces: 29–30, 45, 52, 236–41

Palmas (palmate stones): 151, 165

Pasión river: 74

Patio de los Altares: see Cholula

Payon, García: 123

Pedras Negras: 133

Petén, the: 28, 74

Platforms: 18, 20, 28–29, 33–34, 61–63, 66, 81, 89, 106, 109–10, 116, 126, 130, 139, 146–47, 213, 221–28, 234; at El Tajín, 156–59, 169; at Zempoala, 179, 182; at Monte Albán, 189, 199–200, 203, 207

Plazas: 4, 28–29, 33, 62, 109–10, 234; at Cholula, 63; at Tula, 75–79; at Xochicalco, 132, 139; at

lula, 59; Tula, 81–88; Tenayuca, 94, 99–103

Tenayuca: 74, 103–104, 106, 109–10; history, 93; pyramids, 93–94, 99–101; and Toltecs, 93–94; and Aztecs, 94, 102–103; superimpositions, 94, 101, 103; stairways, 94, 101–103; Coatlpantli, 94, 99; Tláloc temple, 99–100; Temple of the Sun, 100; ball court, 103

Tenenexpan: 175

Tenochtitlán: Aztec capital, 12, 106, 108, 112, 123; temples, 102, 179, 182, 184; ceremonial center, 111; Temple Mayor, 111; platform, 112

Teopanzolco: 102–103, 106; Aztec ruins, 146–50; ceremonial center, 146; Temple of Quetzalcoatl, 146–47; murals, 147; superimpositions, 147; temples, 147–48, 182; pottery, 148–49

Teotihuacán: 16, 59, 61, 63, 69, 71, 74–75, 77, 92–93, 102, 106, 122, 124, 131, 138, 146, 153, 198–99, 210, 212, 238; architecture, 23, 29–30; population, 23; Pathway of the Dead, 23, 28–33, 37; Pyramid of the Moon, 23–28, 60; Pyramid of the Sun, 24–28; Plaza of the Moon, 28–29, 49, 60, 62; murals, 28, 36–58, 153; Palace, Temple of Quetzalpapalotl, 29, 49–50, 52, 137, 228; Palace, Temple of the Jaguars, 29, 49–50, 52; Cuidadela (Citadel), 33; Great Compound, 33; Pyramid, Temple of Quetzalcoatl, 34, 41, 134; superstructures, 33–34; influence on other cultures, 34–36

Terminal Classic period: 12, 146, 229

Terraces: 21, 122–23, 130, 181

Ticoman: 190

Tikal: 26, 33, 35

Tlacochahuaya: 215

Tlacolula: 213

Tlahuica (ceramics): 149

Tlalixcoyan—Temojadas-Tierra-Blanca area: 151

Tláloc (rain god, god of water): 34, 41–43, 45, 47, 50, 52, 55, 65, 99–100, 138, 147

Tlapacoya: 3–4, 18

Tlatelolco: 102, 147, 182, 190, 195; Toltec architecture, 106; history, 106, 108; commercial center, 108–110; temple platforms, 109–10; twin pyramid complex, 109–10; murals, 110–11; Templo Calendarico, 110–11

Tlatilco: 3–4, 6, 9, 18

Tlohtzin: 94

Toltecs: 12, 33, 61, 74, 82, 84, 92, 103, 122, 131, 136, 143, 147, 182, 229; at Tenayuca, 93–94

Toluca: 113

Tombs: 4, 6, 63, 67–69, 230, 232; at Monte Albán, 40, 104–105, 187, 189, 199, 201, 205, 207, 211–12; vaulted, 195; at Mitla, 219–21, 226; at Yagul, 232, 234–41; at Zaachila, 243–48

Totonac culture, Totonacs: 179, 181, 184

Travel guide to sites: 249–52

Tres Zapotes: 4, 9

Tula: 73, 131, 147, 182, 238; Toltec capital, 12, 74, 122; history, 74–75; ceremonial center, 75–76, 85, 90, 92; Great Plaza, 75–79; Building C, 77; ball courts, 77–78, 88–89, 143; Great Vestibule, 78–80; Temple, Pyramid of Quetzalcoatl (Structure B), 81–88; sculptures, 82–88; the Coatlpantli, 87–88; El Corral, 89–90, 124–26; Atlantean figures, 92–93; murals, 92

Tulum: 73, 137, 166, 212, 227

Uaxactún: 212

Uxmal: 228

Vaillant, G. C.: 148–49

Vault, corbelled: 171

261